MICROCOMPUTERS AND
LANGUAGE ARTS

April lovelace

Open University Press

English, Language, and Education series

General Editor: Anthony Adams

Lecturer in Education, University of Cambridge

This series is concerned with all aspects of language in education
from the primary school to the tertiary sector. Its authors are
experienced educators who examine both principles and practice of
English subject teaching and language across the curriculum in the
context of current educational and societal developments.

TITLES IN THE SERIES

Computers and Literacy
  Daniel Chandler and Stephen Marcus (eds.)
Children Talk About Books: Seeing Themselves as Readers
  Donald Fry
The English Department in a Changing World
  Richard Knott
Microcomputers and the Language Arts
  Brent Robinson

In preparation

English Teaching: Programmes and Policies
  Anthony Adams and Esmor Jones
Teaching Literature for Examinations
  Robert Protherough

MICROCOMPUTERS AND THE LANGUAGE ARTS

Brent Robinson

Open University Press
Milton Keynes · Philadelphia

Open University Press
Open University Educational Enterprises Limited
12 Cofferidge Close
Stony Stratford
Milton Keynes MK11 1BY, England
and
242 Cherry Street
Philadelphia, PA 19106, USA

First Published 1985

British Library Cataloguing in Publication Data

Robinson, Brent
   Microcomputers and the language arts. —
   (English language and education series)
   1. English language — Computer assisted instruction
   2. Microcomputers
   I. Title   II. Series
   420'.7'8   PE1066

   ISBN 0–335–15075–6

Library of Congress Cataloging in Publication Data

Robinson, Brent.
   Microcomputers and the language arts.
   (English, language, and education series)
   Bibliography: p.
   1. Language arts — Computer assisted instruction.
   I. Title.   II. Series.
   LB1576.R63   1985   428'.0028'54   85–11581

   ISBN 0–335–15075–6 (pbk.)

Text design by Clarke Williams

Typeset by Freeman Graphic, Tonbridge, Kent
Printed in Great Britain by St. Edmundsbury Press,
Bury St. Edmunds, Suffolk

To my wife, who first showed me what a computer was; and to my daughter, who constantly reminds me what it isn't.

Contents

General Editor's Introduction

It is a particular pleasure to introduce the present book by Brent Robinson, as he has become a colleague of mine at the University of Cambridge's Department of Education. He wrote the text of the book while still the head of English at a comprehensive school in Winchester.

As his first chapter shows, Brent Robinson is well aware of the practical problems facing the classroom teacher of English who wants to introduce the microcomputer into classroom work. However, the book is in many ways more theoretical in its emphasis than some of the other publications of the Open University Press in this field. This seems to me a timely approach. There have now been a number of books dealing with the introduction of computers into the classroom at a practical level. What has been lacking, until now, is an attempt to put on record the present state of the art at a thoretical level, but in a jargon-free way so that it is accessible to the English teacher whose experience of microcomputers is still limited, possibly to the extent of having looked at or perhaps used a few programs. Such teachers will find that this book speaks directly to them. It grows largely out of the author's own research studies at the University of Southampton and the work that he has done for the Microelectronics Education Programme, and presents a considered statement that is as up-to-date as anything can be in this rapidly changing field.

I have used the term 'English teaching' in the above introduction. The term 'language arts', which Brent Robinson prefers and which Esmor Jones and I also used in our *Teaching Humanities in the Microelectronic Age* (Open University Press, 1983), may need some explanation to English readers, though it is commonly used in Scotland as well as in North America. The word 'English' seems to many of us too inclusive; there is a need for a term to cover the specific concern with language and communications that is for many at the centre of the English curriculum today.

Brent Robinson has shown in his work in program development – notably with Cambridge Language Arts Software Services – (CLASS) that he has a concern with literature; see especially his program *Adverse*, which makes possible the creation of electronic and dynamic text. The focus of this book, however, is primarily on the language and communications side of English teaching. The term 'language arts' is useful in putting the emphasis still firmly on the humanities side of the curriculum, while escaping the inclusivity of the traditional English curriculum in England and Wales.

The implications of the development of microcomputers for the future of literacy are of fundamental and far-reaching importance. The Open University Press has produced an international symposium on this topic in Chandler and Marcus's *Computers and Literacy* (1985) to which Brent Robinson also contributed. *Microcomputers and the Language Arts*, the statement of a personal view by a gifted teacher and researcher, takes the discussion a significant stage further.

We hope in this series to continue to advance the argument, as the implications of microcomputers for language arts teaching and research continue to develop.

Anthony Adams

Introduction

Ever since their advent, computers have become more powerful and at the same time smaller and cheaper. By the end of the 1970s the rapid development of electronic technology was such that schools could realistically consider the purchase of one or more microcomputers. A domestic market had also opened up to give children a potential access to microcomputers at home as well. Like many teachers, I remained ignorant of the medium.

Then, in 1980, I watched my wife, a fellow teacher, keying into her computer a program written by a pupil in her mathematics class, and I come to the sudden and unexpected realisation that here was a medium that could be greatly concerned with language. Previously, I had been aware of computers only as 'number crunchers', executing numerical tasks via a program of instructions given in machine code. As I watched my wife encoding this program, I saw her using an alphanumeric keyboard similar to a conventional typewriter keyboard, and producing a symbolic printed language (in this case on a screen) close enough to English for me to recognise and comprehend in part. When the resulting program was executed, I saw the computer print nothing but natural language statements and questions, to which the user would be prompted to respond in English via the keyboard.

My first notion of computers had been false. Here was a medium using English to communicate – or rather, to interact, since it appeared to be a sustained two-way verbal communication process. As an English teacher, I had to consider this medium more carefully, especially if it was being used by my pupils at home and elsewhere in school, making language demands upon them, and if as we are constantly being reminded, computers in one form or another are likely to be increasingly important in their future.

Certain questions immediately arose to a computer illiterate like me. To what extent were computers programmed to 'use' recognisable English? In what ways could they use it? Would they continue to do so? These were naïve questions, revealing that I did not really understand the characteristics of the medium, especially the ways microcomputers functioned. My queries also hinted at some complex issues that are still highly problematic today. We cannot offer many definitive statements in this field, nor can we predict with accuracy what lies ahead, but we can look at current trends and recent developments. There is, for instance, a recognisable search for 'user-friendly' computers. One way of achieving ease of interaction between computers and users has been to develop high level programming languages. Machine code, the language in which computers operate, is low level and consists in essence of nothing more than a series of numbered codes. It is meaningless to anyone other than a programmer. The nearer a programming language approximates to English, the more high level it is. BASIC (Beginners' All Purpose Symbolic Instruction Code) is a high level language, the same one I watched my wife using on that first encounter with a microcomputer. I now use computer software written in Prolog (PROgramming in LOGic), which is nearer to the syntax and semantics of written English. In the future, it is predicted that the new generation of microcomputers being developed in Japan for the 1990s will employ a development of this in a bid to become even more user-friendly, communicating with users in their native language.

The interaction between computer and user is not confined solely to programming. In many circumstances, the tasks are already specified and a computer is pre-programmed to execute them. Whether it is a particular learning experience for a pupil in school, or a data-processing operation for an office manager, for example, the user will need to address the computer to perform the task and, as the machine does so, to be addressed by it. Teachers of the language arts ought therefore to consider if language has a role in this new medium; and, if it does, to ensure that pupils are prepared to cope with the probable linguistic demands.

Computers and language

Language arts teachers need to be concerned not solely with the potential for linguistic interaction between computer and user, but also with its possible function. A computer is a device for handling or processing information. Much of this is to do with numbers because so much of the information in the world is numeric; but numbers are themselves only concepts that have been encoded for convenience. When they are fed into a computer, they are themselves coded yet again in whatever form any particular machine is constructed to work with. In the case of most computers today, this is a series of binary 'switches' of some kind. Equally, letters and words are merely coded concepts, and they too can easily be re-coded so that a computer can handle them. It ought to be possible to employ a computer efficiently to perform completely or in part a number of the linguistic routines traditionally assigned to human users. Word processing is a typical example, while the increasing efficiency and sophistication of this and other electronic information retrieval systems call into question the place and limit of school instruction in alphabetical ordering, sequencing, indexing and referencing of material. Pupils will need to be taught the concepts and rehearsed in the means of directing computers to perform these tasks for them. This might call for a shift of emphasis in the language skills now taught in schools; it will certainly call for new skills to be taught. It might even call for new concepts of literacy and oracy.

There ought also to be a place for microcomputers in what is already taught in the language arts. In being programmed to communicate verbally, computers can call for the exercise of many language skills among users. They can also be expressly programmed to exercise specific language skills, making use of their ability to process language to demonstrate such processes, to stimulate thought and expression or to match user performance against computer.

To take an example, much language learning concerns initial demonstration and subsequent practice. Computers are a suitable medium for this in that they can provide graphics, colour, animation and sound to present language, to manipulate, analyse and synthesise it and to contextualise it with pictures and sounds. A microcomputer in a classroom can become an electronic blackboard for the presentation itself, or it can become a control device for a presentation from a diversity of sources (like audio tape recorders or video and compact disk players). A microcomputer can be utilised not only for initial presentation but also for subsequent practice. Users can interact with a microcomputer through a keyboard or through an increasing range of other devices (for example, light-pens, joysticks and touch-sensitive tablets); spoken interaction is also likely in the future. In all cases, a microcomputer can provide a degree of individual attention, immediate reinforcement, privacy, meticulousness and consistency of performance where a teacher often cannot.

'Teaching machines'

This is not the first time that teaching machines have been proposed for use in the language arts curriculum. In the late 1950s and 1960s, teaching machines could be found in some classrooms. They varied enormously. Some resembled television receivers with electronically switchable projectors that could handle a sequence of slides featuring pictures or text of some kind. In more advanced designs, the carousels were replaced by film strips that could be displayed frame by frame, or even by brief cine sequences. In some cases, a sound track was added. A pupil sat in front of all this, responding to questions on a screen by pushing one of a small range of buttons.

It is important today to distinguish between such machines and computers. In practical terms, the early teaching machines were inefficient and unreliable. The more dynamic they tried to be and the more varied in output (text, graphics, film, sound, etc.), the more mechanical they became, the more intricate in design and the more prone to breakdown.

Computers can also be used as mechanisms to control other devices. Indeed, as I shall later discuss, there are still some presentations of language material like spoken speech and live action motion sequences that computers cannot really undertake on their own and where sound and video tape or disk are still really necessary for storage and retrieval. But use a computer to control these devices and learning is immediately enhanced. The interfacing of these devices with a computer can now rely on electronic rather than mechanical technology. This increases reliability and efficiency. Even those mechanical parts of the integrated system that do remain in use will gradually be replaced as more solid state technology is developed and as computers increase their own capacity to store and present the animation, live motion and human speech that we may obtain only via other devices at present.

In interaction, too, it is important to distinguish between early mechanical teaching machines and computers. The dynamic attribute of the former was largely illusory. True, at each step of the process pupils had a choice – sometimes of three or more possible courses for action – but this was barely enough to encompass the diversity of thought and response that users were likely, and might often be encouraged, to make. It was impossible to eliminate the lucky guess element that enabled effectively untaught users to advance beyond their level of understanding. Whenever the incorrect button was depressed, each user tended to come up against a simple error message before being returned to the previous decision point. There was little opportunity for lengthy re-mediation loops or flexible branching according to user performance.

Learning theory

There were other reasons why these early teaching machines were rejected by teachers, particularly in Britain. Their design and introduction were largely motivated by the work of the Harvard University psychologist B. F. Skinner, who stressed the importance of rewarding correct responses and punishing – or, at least, not rewarding – incorrect ones. This accorded well with the precedent set by the linguist Leonard Bloomfield. Bloomfield began with the proposition that speech was primary and writing secondary. In his analysis of speech, he saw features similar to those of the 'stimulus and response' theory in psychology. One speaker's utterance acted as a stimulus to the hearer, whose reply formed a response to that stimulus.

For Bloomfield, the study of language was to be rigorous and scientific: meaning was so elusive, so difficult to observe, so inaccessible to structural analysis, so mentalistic, that it was not appropriate as the subject of a scientific methodology. By the late 1950s, an established methodology of language teaching had grown up in the United States; it was based on Bloomfield's structuralist linguistics as far as its language content was concerned, and on behaviourist psychology (in particular on stimulus–response conditioning theory) as far as its principles of language and teaching were concerned. Teaching became essentially mechanistic in its approach, replicating with human learners the conditioning and habit-forming techniques that had proved so successful in animal training experiments. Learning became 'over-learning'; hence pattern/practice drills of inordinate length. Meaning became subordinate to mimicry and memorisation. In such a context, mechanical teaching aids found a ready home.

Some teachers, particularly those in Britain, preferred the theories of Piaget to those of Skinner; behaviourist theories of learning never found acceptance among them. Skinnerian psychology was rejected, as were the pedagogic methodologies and teaching aids based upon it. In the United States too, Noam Chomsky attacked the Bloomfieldian school of linguistics and the methodology of language teaching derived from it. Chomsky argued that behaviourism itself was suspect: 'It seems that there is neither empirical evidence nor any known argument to support any specific claim about the relative importance of "feedback" from the environment and the "independent contribution of the organism" in the process of language learning.'[1]

Chomsky tended to the view that all children have some inbred language acquisition device enabling them to process the language data they hear so as to reproduce and build upon it. It is this creative ability in language that the behaviourist theory of language acquisition does not account for. More than this, if Chomsky's view is correct, it may be that the conscious mental processes of the learner can be called upon to facilitate his or her acquisition of new language material. So we might seek out a method of language teaching that would incorporate this fact. Chomsky's theories are far more in tune with modern language arts methodology than Bloomfield's ever were. His approach is assumed in terms like 'cognitive code learning' or 'conscious rule generalisation'.

Creativity

Does this mean that computers must be rejected in the language arts curriculum as their mechanical predecessors were, despite the improvement in performance? The answer, I believe, is no. Unlike their earlier counterparts, computers are not devices solely to be found in teaching. They have a flexibility of function limited only by the range of programs that may be written for them. The same microcomputer that a pupil might use in class can be found performing a range of functions in commerce, industry, administration, research and a variety of other situations. Our future citizens need to be prepared to meet the machines and to cope with the linguistic demands they make. At the same time, the flexibility of function that computers possess means that the machines need not be confined in school simply to presentation or drill and practice routines. Computers can be programmed to present a range of language activities where the emphasis need not only be upon the establishment of good language habits, but can be upon the development of cognitive activities for the exploration of language, thought and the external world.

Some of the programs we devise might still consider language mechanically and/or in isolation – that is, in small units divorced from longer utterances and/or removed from wider semantic or situational frames of reference. There is a place for this, particularly in the remediation of language problems. On the other hand, English is not concerned solely with language as code. As a process of communication it involves semantic components, sustained texts and situations for use. The language arts also involve imagination and creativity both in pupils' own efforts and in the appreciation of the language of others, notably in literature. Literature demands other aesthetic considerations such as an awareness of character, plot, style and theme. Computers may not be applicable to the whole language arts curriculum but they certainly are to a large proportion of it. In language teaching they can be programmed to extend this open-ended communication involving, for example, problem solving, simulation and a range of other less prescriptive, more imaginative language and learning activities. In literature, microcomputers can provide new interactive strategies for readers in their engagement with texts. In both language and literature, microcomputers could even lead to a wider use of electronic technology for linguistic composition, storage and subsequent presentation of texts. The result could be new and extended textual art forms with considerable implications for what is now taught.

The microcomputer is no *deus ex machina*, and the advent of these machines is likely to engender as many problems as opportunities. It may be that microcomputers will allow teachers to implement more effectively certain activities that they have always offered children. The presence of the machine might also prompt teachers to attempt yet more or present language arts activities differently. There will be things a microcomputer cannot do as well as a teacher (with or without present resources) and things a microcomputer can do but a teacher will not. Machines should not distort methodology but extend it. The following chapters explore some of the ways in which that extension may proceed.

The shape of this book

There may be issues in this field that are new to many teachers of the language arts. To facilitate matters, I have adopted a structure familiar to most teachers of the subject. The book divides the language arts into four skill areas: reading, writing, talking and listening; and applies the skills to both language and literature. We examine some of the applications and implications of microcomputer technology and development within each language mode and sphere of activity. Obviously, this is a crude and artificial categorisation of the subject. As language skills, they are all entwined and are often taught or used in class concurrently. (Talking and listening are considered together, for two reasons. Not only does the present state of the art in computer recognition and synthesis of speech limit what might be usefully stated about each; but also the two skills – and the problems computer designers have encountered in tackling them – are very closely akin.) This four-way categorisation is further hampered by the fact that much computer software, just like many other language arts activities, cannot easily be categorised in this way. It implicates and draws upon both reading and writing – as well as, when used in group work, talking and listening skills. Before treating the four skills, we begin in Chapter 1 by exploring the problems in broad terms, before moving on to a more refined evaluation of the particular language modes. Here at the outset we consider the organisational problems that might be encountered when first introducing this software and the new technology generally to a language arts curriculum.

The structure is pragmatic. The book aims simply to explore and suggest how and where a microcomputer might have application or implication in a language arts curriculum. I hope also to reveal some of the strengths and weaknesses of microtechnology in the language arts, and to indicate where present curricula need revision to reflect developments, both present and projected, in electronic technology. What follows may soon be out of date, and the book's projections may prove wayward. I hope, however, that the subsequent pages will form a start for some readers, helping them towards their own informed conclusions on how, where and to what extent microcomputers can and should be used in their own teaching.

1 Practical problems facing language arts teachers

For many teachers it must be difficult to see beyond the practical problems that the new electronic technology appears to pose. It is no good just presenting arguments designed to convince teachers of the support and enrichment that computers can provide, nor explaining to them only the imperative that we teach the skills associated with this new medium. Even teachers already well disposed to the challenge of the technology may see insurmountable practical problems in their path. It seems sensible therefore to consider these problems before moving on to more specific issues related to the aims, objectives and methods of teaching in the language arts curriculum.

Access

The first question is how to gain access to a computer. In normal circumstances, there will already be other departments with some form of computer provision. When setting out, it might be possible to borrow a computer – especially if it is required outside school hours to take home for familiarisation. But this is not the best way of getting to know the potential of the machine. Only when the computer is in use with children can teachers begin to see the possibilities, and the pitfalls, associated with its use.

In some schools it will be impossible to take the computer into the language arts classroom. This is particularly true where a computer network has been installed in a room set aside for the purpose. An advantage of using a network is that all the students can be placed around computers at the same time. There are no awkward problems concerning classroom management and what to do with the rest of the class. A note of caution, however: the thought of serried rows of students communicating in isolation with machines is enough to make some teachers – rightly – recoil in horror. There are times, though,

1

when it can be exciting to have a whole class working on computers simultaneously. Computer provision of this extent can allow for creative writing workshops in which all the students have access to information and word processing facilities. If the computers are interfaced in a network it is even possible to send texts between work stations for comment and amendment in a truly collaborative writing co-operative. At the same time, I would still want pupils to interact more personally and would normally require students to work in groups where they can support each other, learn together and practise socialising and communicating skills.

There will be problems if the only way in which students can gain access to computers is by leaving their classroom. It is important for teachers and students to see computers as just another resource in the class. In the same way that pupils may be directed towards a particular book or worksheet as appropriate, so they might be directed towards a computer. If, for example, a pupil has difficulty with a particular reading or writing skill, a computer could have just the program to demonstrate that skill and provide practice in using it. So the pupil can go off to the corner of the room to load and run the computer before returning to the previous activity. Another pupil might want information on a particular subject for a project. He or she should be able to interrogate the computer for guidance in his or her search, or for presentation of the data itself. Only when the computer is easily accessible can it be used in this flexible way by teachers and be seen by pupils to be a useful resource designed as a tool to work for them.

This is not to advocate a high level of computer provision, which would be impractical in most schools. An adequate, if not ideal, level of provision would be only one computer per class. There will be times when more are required but then it is hoped that others can be borrowed from other classrooms in the department. On the rare occasions when an even higher level of provision is warranted, the class can move to the computer room.

Hardware

The computer is not the only piece of equipment needed. A monitor of some sort is essential. Most computers are designed to operate with conventional television receivers, and this will certainly reduce cost. However, language arts software is going to rely on more than usual amounts of textual display. It is essential that this text is clearly legible. A proper video monitor will give a much sharper and more stable display of text than a conventional television receiver – unless the set has been adapted to take dual radio frequency (RF) and video input signals. It is easy to cut the cost by making do with a second-hand television set, which can be picked up cheaply; but again, these give an inferior RF signal and, if old, might have worn cathode ray tubes or faulty contrast and brightness controls. Any of these faults can create illegible screen displays.

Monochrome displays should also be avoided. Software designers do not give enough care to the colours in which they present text on screen. Some colour combinations of text and background are virtually illegible on colour screens. In monochrome they are impossible to read. There are many variations on the monochrome screen. Today they are not all black with varying shades of white. They may also be amber, green or blue. Coloured text does not always appear clearly on these screens, and I have seen some children work with software in which the colour of the screen totally cancelled out the program text.

The fact that so much language arts software is concerned with text raises important issues concerning the way text is stored. The cheapest way of storing computer programs and any texts or files the programs use is on cassette tape. Unfortunately, this takes a long time to load into the computer. Some programs can take up to seven or eight minutes to load and then still require further loading of a file of text. Pupils cannot wait around that long, or if they do they become impatient and restive. If a computer is turned off accidentally then the whole process has to be repeated. A random-access disk drive can be several times the price of a cassette player but it loads programs and data files in seconds. It also provides immediate access to any part of the disk, so a number of programs or text files can all be available instantaneously on the same disk.

At some stage, it is likely that teacher or students will see the need for a printer. There are a range to choose from but the daisy wheel printer produces the most 'professional' and legible printout. Dot matrix printers are cheaper and faster but they produce each character from a series of dots, and the quality of text, though improving, is still not comparable with that of a daisy wheel printer.

Before buying a printer, a number of questions must be answered. The printer is not as integral to a computer system as the disk drive, monitor and computer itself. Many computer activities do not require a printer and, even when they do, it is often possible to store the text on disk for printing out later when a printer is available. On most occasions, it will be preferable if a printer is not available in the classroom. They are noisy devices. One centrally placed printer will suffice for most needs, and it might often be possible to obtain access to another department's printer at some mutually convenient time. If money is available for extra equipment, thought could first be given to the purchase of some of the other peripheral devices now available for a microcomputer. Young language learners in particular have much to gain from such aids. There are a number of alternatives to the conventional keyboard with its many keys. Some devices have only a few keys but can still produce the full alphanumeric set through the depression of these keys in combination. Touch-sensitive pads allow teachers to devise their own flat keyboards. Light-pens, joysticks and paddles can all facilitate user interaction with a computer and obviate the confusing array of language sub-skills upon which conventional users must draw.

Even an elementary level of equipment provision cannot be achieved immediately. In fact, it might be difficult to raise any money at all. There is often incredulity, ignorance and scepticism in the minds of head-teacher, other staff, parent associations and even pupils when teachers of the language arts say that they want to introduce computers in their subject. Often it is the more literate and more articulate hearers who are quickest to respond. They cannot see what machines have to do with the traditional language skills and literary experiences they associate with, and wish to preserve in, the language arts. A good amount of persuasive groundwork has to be done here.

Deployment

What happens to the first computer? It would be invidious to place it within one classroom for that teacher's sole use. On the other hand, sharing it around would give no pupil adequate 'hands-on' experience. My solution would be to place it in a library or resource centre. With appropriate software, it can be deployed as an information retrieval and resource cataloguing system so that both students and staff immediately see the technology has serious everyday applications. At the same time, it would be freely available for individuals and for small groups of students who are sent by various teachers to run specific tutorial software upon it according to their needs. The machine would also be available to staff in free moments for their own familiarisation with both the hardware and the software (probably stored in the resource centre) available to run on it. As more computers can be purchased, so each individual teaching classroom can be equipped until there are sufficient machines for most language arts needs.

As soon as a computer is introduced into a classroom there will be problems to be overcome. An immediate question is the siting of the machine. Bright artificial light sources or windows make computer screens difficult to read. Computers are robust, but chalk and other dust can make them behave erratically. In any case it is unlikely that a teacher will want to place the computer near a blackboard, the focus of class attention. On the other hand, computers are novel, eye-catching and noisy machines. Good software allows the teacher to turn off the sound but the display is still colourful and dynamic. Careful siting will be needed if the machine is not to form a constant source of distraction for the class.

Siting will also be important for other considerations. A major advantage of the computer is that it can be used for remedial tuition by individual students. Inconsiderate placing of the machine will expose the user to class scrutiny. Instead, the remedial pupil needs the privacy to work quietly, assured by the seclusion and freedom from censure that good tutorial software on a computer can give.

Far more problematic is the challenge that computers provide to teaching styles. Unlike most other resources, computers are dynamic and interactive. They employ teaching and learning strategies that might militate against those already found in the classroom. Software varies so much in design that both traditional and modern teachers may find difficulty in integrating particular programs into their curricula. Just as important, the students themselves might find adjustment difficult if a specific program employs a learning or teaching strategy for which they have not been fully prepared. Even if the software does not create any problems, the fact that only a few pupils can access the computer at any one time calls for styles of teaching that many teachers have yet to adopt. Where classrooms have broken away from formal, whole class teaching, computer deployment is less problematic; classes used to individualised resource-based learning will find computers easier to accept. Teachers who already use group work will find no difficulty in allowing one group to access the computer while engaging the rest of the class in other purposeful activity.

Because of the difficulties, senior teachers may also be faced with a number of management issues. I have already mentioned the problem of finance and the initial priming that might be needed before any money is forthcoming. Even when the money is available, decisions will have to be made concerning the exact type and level of provision. It will be important to bear in mind any policy decisions that have already been made concerning standardisation. This can operate at national, local or school level. Certain constraints will be immovable and, even where there is room for deviation, careful thought must be given to compatibility if resources are to be shared or borrowed from elsewhere. To begin with, it is unlikely that many departments will be able to afford anything but a basic system: computer, monitor and disk drive. Yet there will be times when a printer or second disk drive will be valuable. It is no good borrowing the equipment from another department, school or teachers' support centre only to find that it is totally incompatible with the equipment already possessed.

Implementation and teacher roles

There might be policy decisions of another sort that the departmental head will have to acknowledge in introducing computers. The use of computers anywhere in a school curriculum is likely to implicate school attitudes to curriculum development and electronic technology. It will also relate to school policies concerning resource-based learning, the role of language in learning, study skills and interpersonal communications. Computers can be badly utilised just like any other resource. For the head of a language arts department or for any teacher responsible for language development, it is important to be aware how computers are being utilised elsewhere in the curriculum.

Computers use language extensively: they can store, retrieve and display large amounts of it, making considerable demands in terms of reading and study skills. They make explicit use of language in the interactive learning and teaching strategies they employ. They can create language environments around themselves as they are used in class. Many of the language situations and tasks now being created by computers are those that enlightened language teachers have been urging their colleagues to adopt for a number of years. On the other hand, some are more invidious. There will be occasions when the language arts teacher can offer specific advice to colleagues about the way computers ought to be used in their classrooms.

Within the language arts department, the departmental head might encounter other problems. Staff will react to the introduction of microtechnology in various ways; not all of their responses will be expected. With a scarce resource, the teacher who is resistant to innovation has an excuse for magnanimously declining to take the new technology on board. In contrast, another teacher who is known to be traditional in methodology may be only too eager to obtain a machine. It is easy to see why: the motivating power of the medium is such that students will accept almost any teaching style or content on it. Provide a lively game with plenty of action and even the most boring and arid drill and practice activity will be enthusiastically received by students. The teacher might even be reassured that this way of teaching was right all along. Dynamic conservatism can be revealed in a host of ways. Senior teachers should be constantly vigilant that this expensive resource is being used in wise and educationally appropriate ways that maximise its potential.

Successful implementation of the new technology will arise only if teachers are given full support. There must be a commitment to initial training followed by the provision of a strong support service to resolve problems that ensue. The degree of difficulty that teachers can experience in adapting to the technology should not be underestimated. In running in-service training courses for teachers, I constantly find their discussion moves away from computers themselves to questions more deeply concerned with the fundamentals of teaching a language arts curriculum. The new technology asks us to reconsider the skills within that curriculum and the relative value of each. It asks us to reconsider the balance we maintain between the four language modes. As I hope to show, it is also likely soon to ask us to reconsider our very definition of literacy and our concept of literature. Not only is the content of the curriculum affected; our methods for imparting that curriculum are also queried by the fact that the resource itself is interactive, capable of presenting its own pedagogic strategies and requiring integration into existing classrooms.

Acceptance of the new technology also means acceptance of a different teacher role. It will take time to develop. Senior management need to accept that there will be some professional incompetence in the process. They should be prepared to accept this as teachers learn to change and adapt. Students too should be tolerant. It is natural for them not to be. For once, they can see that they have more command of the new technology than their teachers. The normal classroom roles can become totally reversed. This will be no bad thing if students can then take more responsibility for their own learning.

Change will not occur overnight. Teachers cannot hope ever to have mastery over this new resource. They have a responsibility to become proficient in its use both as teachers and as society users. The technology has an awesome development rate, and teachers will continually need to adapt, to harness the power of the medium.

For this reason, teachers ought not to waste their time learning programming. The task is highly labour-intensive, the knowledge acquired soon out-of-date. At one time, do-it-yourself programming was the only way to obtain software. There is now a growing range of software available, some of it of very high quality. Occasionally, it is still useful to be able to change the vocabulary or other data used in a language arts program, but more and more content-free software is appearing on the market. In the language arts, this type of software embodies certain skills and strategies but no data. Users are free to create their own texts and word lists for loading into a computer and using alongside such software. Normally, it is quite easy to create this electronic data through other 'utility' programs. No programming knowledge is needed.

Soon we shall be faced by a new generation of computers which will make present programming skills redundant. The next generation will be totally unlike those we now use. Computers will interact with humans and organise their own internal data in languages approximating far more closely the natural language of the user. 'Artificial intelligence' will make computers even more capable of direct, meaningful, linguistic interaction with users. Once the new technology is accepted, there will have to be provision made for the curriculum to be systematically and regularly reassessed and for continual staff retraining as new needs and demands are felt across the department, the school and society at large.

2 Computers and reading

Computer software is big business. Each week sees the publication of many new programs. Teachers are assailed by programmers and publishers, often former colleagues, who urge the importance of this or that particular program. Among some proponents of the medium, it must be the sheer profit motive that underlies this hard sell. Among others, there is a genuine belief that the present curriculum stands to be enriched by the implementation of computers. The pressures come upon teachers not from the publishers alone but from several other quarters too. Many parents and governors want to see children working with computers. Employers and government stress the need for schools to take account of the new technology in the skills they teach. Senior teachers encourage their staff to respond; junior teachers with an eye to advancement are keen to do so. Schools are hard pressed for money, and yet severe budget restrictions do not necessarily seem to prevent the spread of this innovation.

Screen and page: two distinct media

We need to stand back from this situation. There is no point in buying an expensive computer and highly priced software for use in reading classes if it offers no more than we can already achieve with existing resources and expertise. A program in which the computer simply stores and presents a series of frames of text in sequential fashion is a very expensive, and not very legible, book. Even when programmers begin to exploit the computer's singular potential, most have so far failed to match expectation. Some of the earliest attempts at computer-assisted reading programs were little more than electronic work-books offering simple drill and practice exercises. We should not castigate such uses out of hand; it is important for students to gain a familiarity with electronic print, since our children are likely to have so much recourse to it in later years. Also, for many reluctant readers, electronic print may be the only way in which they will accept a text. Further, there is a place for drill and practice software, since much language acquisition develops best through initial demonstration and subsequent practice. At the right time, at the right place and for the right purpose, a computer can provide a highly efficient, consistent, patient and entertaining means of providing these activities.

The computer is a highly versatile machine. It can meet these demands and more. This is the challenge that faces us. We need to adapt its versatility to the aims of teachers and to the needs of pupils. The ideal software will take full advantage of the computer's capabilities to enrich what teachers already do, and allow them to do more. The effective utilisation of computers for reading purposes will thus need to marry beliefs about reading processes, expertise in its classroom implementation and knowledge about computer technology. Unfortunately, teachers do not yet know enough about the technology so they cannot really begin to implement it.

The fact that the connection between video technology and reading activity will be unfamiliar to many teachers does not arise from the youth of the medium. It testifies more to the reluctance of many teachers, especially in Britain as opposed to North America, to accept technological curriculum innovation. Teachers of humanities and language arts in particular have had a healthy suspicion of things technical. Despite this, the history of our early use of the electronic medium (for educational broadcasting) is peppered with a significant number of reading series that were excellent in their own right and even gained a degree of acceptance by teachers ready to explore the potential of video technology in the classroom. An exploration of the opportunities now offered by a microcomputer-controlled screen could well begin by bearing in mind the experience and familiarity gained by educators and broadcasters in that not ignoble past.

Caleb Gattegno, originator of the *Words in Colour* reading scheme, warmly welcomed the advent of the video screen. Back in 1969 he saw considerable potential in this new technological display medium:

> we have at our disposal ... a screen in which electrons can be commanded to organise themselves according to our wishes for as long as we wish; color on color tubes; various hues of grey on the older black and white tubes; a sound system to convey the sounds we select for as long as we wish.[1]

Gattegno was so enthusiastic that, for him, the video screen became far more than an additional reading aid. In his projected reading scheme, he designated the medium the central resource, superior even to conventional text:

> Since the image on the screen can be acted upon by will and made to follow the instructions of a programer *[sic]* and since the sound part of the

set can also be used at will, we may find that teaching reading is more effectively done on the television medium than anywhere else for all but a very small minority of children.[2]

Gattegno appears to assume a dismissive attitude towards conventional print. Leaving aside the immediately conservative response in defence of books and other conventional print matter that this is likely to elicit from teachers of the language arts, there are other important issues here. We may question the transfer of skills that is assumed to occur when pupils learn to read through the electronic medium. Perhaps the transfer may be seen to exist in part (though we do not have sufficient evidence to support this claim). But there are also particular idiosyncrasies that make the electronic display of print dissimilar to that on paper. This was true of broadcast print material, and is even more true of the dynamic displays of computerised text. It is likely, therefore, that pupils acquire different and possibly novel skills in their access to electronic print. The reading skills demanded and fostered by the two media are not wholly identical and not entirely applicable to both.

The issue is an important one, not just because we are contemplating the use of electronic displays for the acquisition of basic reading skills. Electronically displayed print is no longer just a reading aid for educational use. The substitution of electronic for conventional print has become a reality in many parts of our society. Readers need the skills to be fluent in both print media. There is a real need for children at school to gain familiarity with electronic and paper print technology.

To some extent, the new skills demanded by electronic print displays are symptomatic of the fact that the new medium has presentational limitations. So from this point of view too, we might not be so supportive as Gattegno for the use of microelectronic technology in the teaching of reading. The video screen does have some of the potential about which Gattegno enthused. Computerised displays have further potential we are only just beginning to discover. On the other hand, microcomputer technology also has limitations that we cannot ascribe to broadcast television (and today we must include here recorded television material on video tape and disk). We can ascribe them still less to conventional print. I hope in this chapter to reveal the strengths and weaknesses that microcomputers exhibit in the reading process and so help us come to a considered response to the medium.

The reading process

For the sake of clarity, this chapter develops a linear and hierarchical approach to the discussion of the reading process. I do not wish to imply that reading is actually like this. Reading is a psycholinguistic process in which readers employ a variety of skills to infer a writer's intended meaning. These skills cannot and should not necessarily be taught in isolation, nor are they employed by readers in this way. The cognitive process of inferring meaning from the visual symbols we call print involves both phonic skills and linguistic skills. We do not yet know the precise number of these skills. Some authorities estimate there are over 2,000 sub-skills so highly interdependent that they cannot be considered in isolation – even if we knew which skills were being called upon at any one time by any one reader.

Moreover, reading involves more than just phonic and linguistic skills. We might break down the reading process into theoretical concepts and manageable categories for instructional purposes, but we must not lose sight of the overriding function of reading. Comprehension is at its core. Skilled readers bring to a text a residue of knowledge distilled from past experience. This informs their interpretation of what they read. It also helps them adopt an appropriate reading strategy involving a particular sub-set of reading skills. A fluent close reading of print can be wasteful if it fails to reflect the reader's situation, purpose and function in accessing the text.

The process of reading, then, is diverse and complex. This chapter is intended to present some of the ways computers can be applied to particular aspects of the reading curriculum. It does not present a coherent reading curriculum, but simply suggests some of the ways in which computer technology bears upon a reading curriculum, with examples of theory in practice. Far less am I advocating a computer-oriented reading programme. I hope to prompt those who read this chapter to formulate and devise the ways and means whereby computers may find a place in the reading activities they offer in their classrooms.

Pre-reading skills

Use of graphics facilities

One particular development in computer technology that is improving rapidly is the resolution of computer graphics. Early computer models had very little, if any, graphics display potential. On the first micro-computers, diagrams and images were constructed from simple line drawings or shape blocks that were treated in the same manner as letter characters for display purposes. Today, computers are able to present more refined picture capabilities. Exceedingly fine lines can be drawn and shapes constructed on the screen with fine points or 'pixels'. A high resolution graphics mode has a screen consisting of a grid with many thousand pixel locations. The number of microcomputers with a high resolution graphics mode is increasing. Some microcomputers have a range of graphics modes with different numbers of pixels on each. Even the more modestly priced machines offer some graphics potential and a considerable range of colours. Given the graphics capability of modern microcomputers, there is considerable potential at a number of developmental stages of reading.

Visual acuity is essential for reading to commence. It is not surprising that the microcomputers recommended for British primary schools by the Department of Industry and the Department of Education (via the Microelectronics Education Programme) were the Sinclair Spectrum, the BBC/Acorn Model B and Research Machines Link 480Z computers. These are sophisticated machines reflecting the opinion expressed by the Minister for Information Technology that, for very young learners, colour and graphics should be 'almost essential, though opinion differs on whether this should be high resolution graphics'.[3] Good animation and graphics are likely to hold children and stimulate them far more than static displays, whether of print or pictures.

One need not look far to see how microcomputers might assist pre-readers. The main perceptual skills for reading involve the ability to distinguish foreground from background, the ability to notice differences in shape and size of image and to perceive spatial arrangement. Children's facility in these skills is increasing all around them all the time in the three dimensions of day-to-day experience. To supplement this, there are a number of products commercially available to assist children to acquire these skills in both the three dimensions of normal experience and the two of most graphic and textual display media. But while these concrete media have many attributes to recommend them, they also have some constraints to limit their usefulness. Computers can often score over other two-dimensional media in their capacities for interaction, for storing a large amount of display material, and in their ability to animate and transmute high quality, animated colour graphics. Computers should be seen as both a supplement to, and an extension of, pre-reading resources. It can also be argued that children should develop perceptual skills in the very medium that will form an important part of their graphic and textual communications systems in later years.

Visual games

Many computer programs currently available might assist the development of pre-reading skills. A number of the successful commercial arcade-type games involving graphics could heighten perceptual acuity. Care must be exercised here in that many programs offer violent activities that we may not wish to offer young learners. Some arcade games, however, are exciting, adventurous and even humorous. Stimulated by the ideas and potential shown by these examples, teachers and programmers could devise further programs. Such software needs to be simple in design and does not necessarily demand the fast-moving animated sequences so common in commercial game software. A static display can be more useful in building certain perceptual skills and might facilitate some aspects of early visual discrimination.

Incomplete shapes or pictures could be presented and the user asked to select visually the missing part from a number of other parts shown on the screen. The successful educational television series *Sesame Street* made use of a variation on this in which viewers were asked to distinguish and pair similar shapes. In a game format, the program could take the form of the memory game 'Pelmanism', which has already been programmed for a number of computers. Here, a number of cards or pictures are displayed on the screen, face down to hide the matching pairs. The player turns over two cards, and if they match, the player scores. Matching cards remain face up, but if they do not match, they are turned back again for another pairing attempt. The pairs are typically chosen at random from a store that includes recognisable objects familiar to a young child's experience.

Another example designed specifically for use with physically handicapped children presents the 'odd man out' problem on a computer as a multiple choice selection. Only two keys are used. The first moves an indicator along a list of choices on screen. (Initially, these are a selection of shapes and then words of increasing length.) The second key enters the selection made by the user. More imaginatively, users could be asked to perform a matching or completion exercise as an integral part of a picture-building activity. The completed image could be a static tableau or it could be a picture narrative in real time where a house is built or doll dressed on screen, for example. Visual jigsaws, 'spot the ball' games, mazes, pictures with hidden objects and many more such programs could be developed and utilised to increase perceptual alacrity and forestall some of the problems of letter reversal, mirror imaging and misplacement encountered when learning to read.

Sequencing

A pre-reader also needs to be trained in left-to-right sequencing. Here again, current software consisting of games and puzzles might find a new use before we turn to new and specific software. On the other hand, we also need to contemplate the adverse effects upon pre-readers that might result from some of the present programs children are beginning to use outside the classroom. Where software for the very young employs captions, there are strong reasons for ensuring that symbols appear from left to right and from top to bottom of the screen. (In cultures where print has a different serial alignment, these criteria will change accordingly.) Users would be helped to gain this orientation through a variety of animated sequences where the predominant directional flow is from top left to bottom right of the screen. If these sequences can be interactive, so much the better.

To take an example, Red Riding Hood is trying to find her way from Granny's cottage at the top left of the screen to her own home on the right. There are a number of routes she could take but only one returns her safely. The viewer traces each track across the screen, selects the right one and animates the girl on screen to see if the choice is correct. There could be many variations on the principle. As an aid for early readers who experience difficulty in following written symbols from the end of one line to the beginning of the next, further extended practice could be given with more programs of the same and greater complexity.

Software involving animation or the building of pictures in rows from left to right on consecutive lines across and down the screen could be followed by similar practice with words. Later, when spellings are introduced, each section of the picture could be shown with a letter so that the total image and word are built up from left to right. Board games of the snakes and ladders format would have a role to play too and could be easily adapted for the screen.

User interaction

Some of the software mentioned above could be simply demonstrative. To make full use of the computer, however, it could also be interactive. This creates a major problem for pre-readers if their means of response is a conventional keyboard. Users cannot be dextrous in the use of an alphanumeric keyboard if they are still young enough to have undeveloped manual motor control or if they cannot read the keys. Teachers should be on their guard against software that conveniently forgets this fact. Some software producers are more enlightened in suggesting that effective software for pre-literate users requires the provision of an alternative form of input to the keyboard.

The immediate answer may be far more simple; young user interactions with a computer will benefit from the presence of an adult or older child. The advantages are several: there is the safety factor involved with any equipment powered by electricity; there is also the need for human contact to practise socialising and linguistic skills; a third party is also necessary to mediate the learning process, since the activity offered and the responses made are likely to be more valuable and effective if children are able to 'talk them through'. At this point, the mediator can go so far as keying in the required input to ensure that the computer receives and acknowledges precisely the response intimated by the young user. In fact, there need be no occasion for users to gain any direct hands-on experience themselves. When my young daughter and I run a computer story in words and pictures I have been working on, she simply listens to my narration of the screen text, and watches the screen response (a graphics animation) as I key in whatever decisions she has selected from those she has been told the computer is offering.

This, however, is not the only solution to the problem of pre-literate computer interaction. Nor is it always the ideal solution in terms of children's involvement in the activity, familiarisation with the technology or development in literacy skills. There are a number of alternative ways of direct communication with a computer. If a computer is communicating visually to a pre-literate user then the user's response could be communicated to the computer via some form of attached peripheral device that accepts the user's inability to recognise and depress lettered keys. A few years ago, such devices were undreamt of or very costly; but today, we can select from light-pens, joysticks, paddles, mice, touch-sensitive screens and pads or a number of other devices. Even speech recognition and synthesis, which I consider in detail later, are becoming realistic alternatives to keyboard input.

Such forms of interaction might do more than facilitate pre-literate interaction with a computer. They might also usefully develop a user's motor skills, which would pave the way for a keyboard to be introduced. When introducing a keyboard, the number of keys is best limited by a mask or template placed over them and/or by disabling keys via the software. The remaining operative keys can then be re-defined in the program as necessary to register specific responses. Keys can also be covered with coloured stickers for easy identification. One computer company has already adopted this technique as part of its marketing strategy. The product is a hand-held battery-operated microcomputer. This is truly portable but suffers from a very small and compact keyboard. To alleviate the situation, one section of the keyboard can be designated with special functions (here, the BASIC key words) and the manufacturers provide a template to cover the original symbol depicted on each key. In Britain, cardboard templates for at least one other domestic microcomputer are also now available in chain stores and computer specialist shops. These templates fit over the keys and may be written upon between the keys to identify all or some of them in any way required.

Beginning reading

The elementary stages of reading follow on naturally from reading readiness. This is not to say that reading readiness forms a discrete developmental stage preceding the early stages of reading proper. Rather, readiness should be seen as the initial stage of learning to read, its activities directly related to the introduction of print and to the development of vocabulary, language and cognitive skills.

Letter and word recognition

It is possible to see a natural progression from pre-reading skills of shape identification to later letter recognition, and many of the programs used for pre-reading may be brought into operation at this stage of development simply by the substitution of letters for shapes and images. Now too, letters can be concealed in pictures for the user to identify. One way of introducing the distinctive features of letters is to conceal them completely. Using a small window on screen, children could be allowed to peek at part of the hidden letter. They could then move the window around the screen to see other parts of the letter. If they are still unable to recognise it, they can enlarge the window until, if necessary, the whole character comes into view.

Readers need also to distinguish between letters when they are presented in juxtaposition. They might therefore be presented with a jumble of letters and asked to pick out all the identical shapes they can find. The activity can be presented as a game, becoming progressively more difficult. It might culminate in the differentiation of visually similar letters like *d*, *p* and *b*; or *v* and *w*.

Discrimination between letters of the alphabet is a critical component of letter identification. In our alphabet, the need is to distinguish between the patterns created with the curve, straight line and angle. Simple games and exercises could be developed to encourage awareness of these shapes. A computer display can also animate the letters themselves to demonstrate their distinctive patterns. In so doing, a reader could be asked to supply missing parts of the letter. When a reader confuses letters, colour and animation can be used to point out the important distinguishing features (like the additional curve and downstroke on *m* compared to *n*).

Later still, words with similar outlines ('feed'/'tool'/'lock') could be presented in a variety of discriminatory activities. In some of these programs, the computer and screen together could replicate electronically the mechanism of the tachistoscope. This presentational device incorporates the flash card reading technique in which a letter, word or sentence is given a brief exposure. Viewers are then asked to identify the letter or word from among a number of distractors or, in the case of sentences, to answer a question on what they have read. When pupils have memorised letter shapes, further computer activities can be designed to reinforce memorisation. One software example 'hides' a selection of letters randomly on screen. Users then uncover them in correct alphabetical order against the clock. If an incorrect input is given, all the letters are hidden once more and the game starts again.

In all such word recognition programs, colour and animation will be useful to highlight or make letters appear, disappear, move around the screen or change shape. As with letter differentiation, these facilities are unique adjuncts of this particular reading resource and would be most advantageous to readers who constantly display word recognition problems like letter omission ('pilot'/'plot'), reversal ('dog'/'god') or substitution ('wish'/'wash').

Meaning and word usage

While programs of this sort can contribute towards effective and rapid recognition of letters and words, they do little to draw readers' attention to meaning or to word usage. This is not to say that a computer cannot contextualise letters and words. In the television series *Sesame Street*, animation has been used to transform a letter into a related word or object and back again. A computer can not only duplicate such demonstrations, but make the activity interactive. A picture of an object can be created on the screen with the initial letter incorporated into the picture. An *S* shape depicted as a snake is an obvious example. Programs might then present the image and prompt a user to depress an appropriate key to complete the picture. Thus all but the first letter of 'snake' appear in a serpentine form, and depression of the *S* key summons the head (or tail) to complete the picture.

Many modern reading schemes have been based upon whole words rather than upon letters or syllables. They deal later with problems of specific letter differentiation. In these curricula, words are related to the objects they represent, and a visual display unit can be used effectively to bridge this gap between objects or non-verbal concepts and the symbolism of the printed word. This technique was used effectively by the BBC's series *Look and read*. Each broadcast programme contained one episode from a continuing serial with significant words imposed on the screen as they occurred in the action. Once viewers had seen each word with its visual referent, the words were shown first on their own and then with a still picture to remind viewers of the context.

This technique is particularly suited to television, which is able to present sequences of live action and accompanying sound. Computer graphics and sound cannot begin to rival the presentational quality of television in this respect. Yet, since computer technology is advancing rapidly, in the future it is likely that computers will be able to store and display large amounts of high resolution animated pictures. It is even more likely (and already possible) that computers will be interfaced with video disk machines to permit the integration of computer program and filmed live action and text stored on disk. Given the resources, it is possible to prepare software reading material that includes the super-imposition of picture and text so that the one adds meaning to the other.

Far simpler techniques are just as relevant and certainly less costly or complex in mechanical installation and operation. Pictures of objects or actions frozen in performance or with limited movement might be shown together with a word and users asked to decide if the word accurately describes the object or action displayed. Users might be asked to select from a choice of words or simply be prompted to supply the word from memory and experience. This is especially appropriate where a program initially presents a run through of such captions or images before the user is asked to select; or where a program utilises a reinforcing program loop repeating information already revealed.

In the first category, an early Pelmanism-type program challenged users to match four object pictures with four referents. A more elaborate version of it could involve the substitution of words for pictures. A word would be shown at the top of the screen and again at the bottom but this time in conjunction with others of similar graphic representation to act as distractors. In giving the correct answer, the word would be supplemented with a picture of the normal object to confirm meaning and to reinforce the learner's correct identification of the word shape.

In the second category, a recent program produced in Britain relies far more on memory and experience. The program builds a full colour picture of a stylised house. Beginning with a blank screen, the house is constructed with four windows, a door, a chimney (complete with animated smoke), a tree-shaded and fenced garden and, finally, a car that drives across the screen to halt in front of the house. As each referent is added to the picture, its name appears in the top left of the screen. Then, when the picture is complete, the screen is cleared. The picture is built up again, but this time the user is prompted to key in the name of each object from memory as it appears.

Keyboard familiarisation and alphabet skills

In programs like this, users are already beginning to use an alphanumeric keyboard. Indeed, it may be that utilisation of a computer for the development of early reading skills causes both letter identification and competence with a keyboard to go hand in hand. At this stage, however, a teacher might consider two alternative strategies. Are the pupils to be introduced directly to a 'qwerty' keyboard or should they be presented with an alphabetically arranged keyboard? The latter might reduce confusion, reinforce alphabetical ordering and improve compatibility with an increasing number of other electronic learning aids that use an alphabetical key pad. Should a teacher wish to adopt this strategy, a mask or stickers can be placed over keys provided that the software allows the function of the keys to be redefined.

Whichever keyboard is considered appropriate, children will need some familiarisation with it. The programs we are considering here might assist letter recognition and familiarisation with the keyboard.

They are also likely to assist in the transfer from an alphabetical to a qwerty keyboard where both are used in succession as a child's reading ability progresses.

There are a number of programs already available for rehearsing alphabetical skills and keyboard familiarisation. The reason for their existence, as with so much software, is not that the concepts such software embodies are seen as educationally imperative. Rather, it is the case that the activities lend themselves easily to programming. In this particular case, however, it is interesting that the target user for some of this keyboard software is a very young user aged four to six. Presumably the manufacturers have noticed that so much software demands keyboard skills from even the youngest age group and so they see an urgency for young users to gain such skills. On the other hand, experience reveals that a large number of early users have sufficient motivation from the medium to master the keyboard very early without any overt instruction. Perhaps, then, the manufacturers might be appealing more to parental desire. Many parents seem to buy a computer to accelerate their child's education progress or even to compensate for the skills of tomorrow for which they see no school provision.

Programs to facilitate alphabetical skills rely on the user's ability to relate screen image to keyboard symbol. An object might be displayed on the screen together with its name. The user has then to copy the word by pressing appropriate keys. In developing such software, it is strange that many of the designers seem to show no consideration for the problems inherent in this matching process. Most computer keys carry upper-case letters. The obvious response from programmers is to use upper-case characters on screen. This cannot be recommended for early readers. Letters and words in upper case are not as easily perceived as those in lower case. Upper-case characters are more closely regimented in size and shape. The visual clues necessary for decoding are neither so distinctive nor so abundant. The response must be to use lower-case characters on screen. Then, if the key symbols are to correspond with the screen characters, the keys will need to be covered by a template or set of adhesive labels bearing lower-case letters. At a later stage, the stickers can be removed to expose the upper-case symbols depicted on the keys. At this point, the characters on screen ought to be upper case. Finally, the screen characters could revert to lower case again, so that users become adept at recognising both upper- and lower-case variants of the same alphabetical letter. What teachers need, therefore, is software that allows them to alternate between upper and lower case as each situation dictates. Few programs currently on the market offer this facility.

While we are considering the display of text, we should not forget that computer graphics also have a role to play here. The graphics potential of most microcomputers available today is arguably one of the most advantageous features of the medium for reading purposes. There is considerable potential in a computer's ability to highlight graphic features of language, synthesising them or breaking them down, categorising and grouping them, demonstrating normally non-visual features and contextualising graphic manifestations of language with objects and situations they represent. A microcomputer in a reading classroom could provide opportunities for activities that were unavailable to teachers in the past or were offered by other media in a less exciting, arresting, manipulable or concise manner. In addition, graphics and animation are particularly attractive to learners, especially the very young and the less able with their short attention spans and less well-developed powers of observation and concentration.

Phonics and computer sound

Phonics are central to the teaching of reading, so some thought needs to be given to computer sound as well as graphics. Gattegno based his own video reading course on the premise that 'On the screen it is possible to animate designs that can be associated with specific sounds'[4], and it is worth looking briefly at how he believed sound and graphics in combination could form a powerful reading aid. Using colour, animation and sound, he presented a scenario for video sequences in which words split apart on the screen with their sounds isolated and identified. He then rejoined them to show how sounds and symbols combine to make spoken and written words. He made letters appear and disappear, move about the screen and rearrange themselves in different settings; with sound accompaniment, he demonstrated how letters vary in sound and value according to their lexical context.

Sherrington[5] was another pioneer who postulated a role for the video screen in reading instruction. He advocated a wider contextualisation of language, suggesting that a sound narration of a story might be accompanied by a display of words on the screen. This was to be more than a broadcast book. In each narration, specific sound/symbol relationships were to be highlighted. Whenever words incorporating such sound elements occurred in the story (so contextualising them and giving them meaning) they also appeared on the screen with the specified sound symbols in each word appearing immediately under each other in a column. This procedure was to be graded so that sound symbols were shown first in an initial position, then medial, then final and ultimately in any position in a word. The words could be further supplemented and contextualised by illustrations, the words superimposed upon the picture or to one side of the screen and appearing one by one.

From a one-to-one symbol-to-sound correspondence, Sherrington proposed that subsequent attention could be given to symbols that are used for more than one sound; or to sounds for which there is more than one symbol. Other features that could be handled similarly, he suggested, were items like prefixes, suffixes, inflectional endings, the silent *e* and unexploded plosives. Following on the contextualisation of such features, Sherrington recommends they may be recapitulated individually or together to highlight salient features with the symbol underlined and the word repeated in the sound channel. The material may then be tested by the presentation of multiple spellings and the sound repeated. After a correct user input all but the correct spelling could dissolve and a confirming picture could appear accompanied by a reinforcing repetition of the pronunciation. At a later stage, a learner might be asked to state whether the sound accompanying a list of words is the same or different. Another exercise might present a number of pictures, each demonstrating a superimposed word with a learner selecting the word with the dissimilar emphasised sound.

Unfortunately, these examples of some of the ways in which sound might be used in early reading development were proposed for a television screen rather than for a computer-driven video display unit. We are not yet at the stage where we can implement such strategies on a microcomputer, for computerised reproduction of human speech is still in its early stages of development. Because letters represent sound, some form of speech output is essential for some early reading computer programs. Yet because of the technological limitations, few computer programs designed to introduce the letters of the alphabet, for example, are able to teach the letter sound or name along with its visual form.

Some software exhibits ingenuity in avoiding the problems of non-vocalised phonics teaching. In one approach, a picture is displayed along with four letters, one of which represents the initial sound of the picture's name. This reduces phonics to matching a picture label with its initial letter and works adequately if the pictures are clear and unambiguous. Sound-matching activities sometimes use a similar approach. In some, the user picks from a group of words the one containing the same sound as the target word. Sometimes it might be initial word sounds, at other times medial vowel sounds, final sounds or rhymes. Despite finding a limited place for such software in the reading curriculum, it cannot be denied that beginning reading is closely linked to a child's oral language. The majority of modern reading methods assume and build upon the relationship between print and oral vocabulary. For a computer to be a really effective teaching tool for those who are not yet proficient readers, it would need to employ sound as well as text.

The Talking Typewriter

The Talking Typewriter was a very early approach to alphabet learning, which began to show how effective (though in this case simple) a reading resource a computer with speech synthesis could be. This device prints letters using large type while at the same time prounouncing both the sound and the name of the letters pressed. Children first gain hands-on experience with the device through a free-ranging exploration of its keys. When the initial novelty palls, the computer asks the user to locate specific letters. Again, users are free to explore various keys in the search but the computer ignores all incorrect responses, repeating the letter name and writing it to screen only when it is successfully located. After locating individual letters, the user moves on to words and then on to the reading and writing of longer prose.

An essential characteristic of the talking typewriter is the fact that it is a responsive device. This was significant to its inventor, O. K. Moore:

> An early example of a simple responsive device is the lyre. One does not ask how efficient a lyre is, as if it were a lever or pulley; one does not ask about a lyre's fidelity as if it were a reproducer, say a phonograph. Instead, the kinds of questions one should ask about a lyre and the Talking Typewriter, too, are: 'Do they foster emotional–cognitive growth?' 'Are they fun to "play" with?' What I am suggesting is that whereas most of those concerned with computers two decades ago conceived of them as highly efficient and faithful master clerks, we were trying to show their potential for enhancing human growth, especially the kind of growth that arises out of playfulness.[6]

The Talking Typewriter is very different to most of the other reading software available. It is not just that it demonstrates the added attribute of speech synthesis. Its design also reveals an important underlying concept at variance with that implicit in much other software. The Talking Typewriter eschews conventional drill and practice strategies and encourages users to take command of the learning situation. It urges them to play with language at whatever level of difficulty they dictate. Incorrect user responses are treated not as errors but as the basis for feedback to the user and further action.

Compared to the Talking Typewriter, much present reading software is second rate. Without an auditory component, the activities incorporated often consist of little more than drill matching of a shape on the screen to a corresponding key. Such software fails to teach the phonemic role of letters in reading experience.

Audio output

A number of attempts have been made to provide the necessary audio output for reading software. One of the easiest sources of acceptable phonics for use in conjunction with a microcomputer is still an audio tape, for it is possible to make use of an audio tape recorder or player remotely controlled by a computer. With many microcomputers, it is a simple matter for a program to control a cassette recorder motor. In some cases, there is no reason why the same cassette deck used for loading and saving programs cannot also be used for the playback of prerecorded sound tapes provided that the recorder has an internal loudspeaker. This sound could be laid down on a cassette immediately after the recording of the data, so that, once a cassette has been placed in the cassette deck and played to load its program, it would be in the correct position for sound replay. Alternatively a new cassette could be inserted to replace that containing the program. The cassette would then be brought into play as the program runs, the motor alternately starting and stopping under program control.

Some computers offer a 'sound through' facility. This allows the playback through a television loudspeaker of ordinary sound recordings stored on a cassette together with the program. Some foreign language software exploits this facility, and there are also some interactive story-books using the same system. These combine animated graphics and accompanying sound narration with occasional pauses for some inter-active game or on-screen task associated with the story-line. At the moment, these examples of interactive fiction rely on pictures and sounds, but the same facility could also use text rather than images or include captions to accompany the visual display and/or sound track.

The main disadvantage of this audio method is that the sound information is stored sequentially on the magnetic tape. Given that microcomputers generally sense and control only the play function of the motor, all audio information to be used must be stored and retrieved in strict linear fashion. A program would not be able to branch to retrieve sound information from any part of an audio tape other than the one following next. The program could not skip over segments of sound track unnecessary for a quick learner, nor regress to an earlier part of the tape for a learner in difficulty. Nor could a program enter a reinforcing loop if that routine required a repetition of parts of the sound track. More versatile in this respect is the interfacing of computer and video disk. Very precise random access offers all these interactive possibilities, provides high quality sound (in stereo or as two concurrent, switchable sound tracks) and also presents excellent visuals – of both text and image. The new compact audio disk offers similar facilities for sound.

In the United States, the widely used PLATO Early Reading Curriculum Project of the mid-1970s made use of random access audio devices. Its SWAT program presented words simultaneously in the sound channel and on screen. The screen also contained other distractor words, and users were prompted to indicate their recognition of the candidate words by using a light-pen. In a more sophisticated version of the software, users had to complete a sentence on screen by selecting an appropriate word from a set that included the target word and a number of distractors. The sentence was also heard in the sound channel with a bleep substituted for the gap. At a higher language level, short stories were presented, the text appearing frame by frame on the screen while users listened to a synchronised audio narration. An arrow moved down the left side of the text to guide readers and the machine stopped at the end of each line. A reader could then choose whether to read the same line again or move on to the next. On the second reading, the user was expected to read along with a narrator. On the third, the computer assisted the reader only if the reader indicated a desire for this on reaching the beginning of each line.

Speech generation and recognition

The problem with video and audio random access disks is that they require special players interfaced with a microcomputer. This makes the system complex and expensive. They also fail to allow teachers to record their own material. We are therefore forced back upon the production of synthetic speech by computer. In its most versatile form, a computer can be programmed to generate speech compiled from phonemes. In theory, an unlimited vocabulary is possible from the small number of phonemes that constitute all the possible words in the English language. In practice, synthetic speech is still of mediocre intelligibility and limited in inflection and tone. These are significant defects when the resource is contemplated for assisting phonic work or developing reading fluency.

How long it will be before a computer can generate synthetic speech of a standard sufficiently worthy to assist an early reader is difficult to determine. It is unlikely to be too far away since there is already hardware that creates speech in primitive form. A number of speech synthesiser modules can be bought quite cheaply for use with the majority of popular microcomputers. Some computers can now be fitted with an integral speech chip. Using an inbuilt speech synthesiser resident in one microcomputer, a hardware manufacturer has produced some early reading cartridges that combine animated colour graphics, captions and computerised synthesised speech.

Speech recognition would also be a useful asset in reading software. It could be used to monitor proficiency in reading aloud the words presented on screen, and could also offer oral rather than graphic response, enabling teachers to divorce reading from spelling. Too often, the input required of even early reading programs necessitates an ability to spell input correctly. Unfortunately, speech recognition is farther away than speech synthesis. Most current voice-entry devices recognise only a small set of less than 100 spoken words. They need also to be tuned to the voice pattern of each individual user.

While the present implementation of computerised sound input and output is limited, the future development of speech synthesis and recognition could greatly enhance the versatility of this medium for reading purposes. It is likely that both sound and a highly manipulable video screen will one day combine to enhance the teaching of reading – though it is perhaps ironic that such developments might in themselves reduce the very need for pupils to read, or write, in their future lives.

Print on video screens

As readers develop their skills, they will need, and probably demand, larger and larger amounts of text to explore with their new-found and developing skills. In software, the visual images generated by a computer's graphics capabilities are likely to be superseded by recognisable letters in the form of continuous text. There are a number of important issues here deserving consideration, though not all of them are immediately obvious.

The graphics potential of a computer is at once novel and unexpected. It immediately demands attention and can be quickly appreciated to offer both reader and teacher opportunities that conventional print cannot. But once a computer is used to display frames of print, it is easy to suppose that the skills involved in reading that print can be transferred directly from the typewritten page. It is easy to assume that the medium no longer offers any particular gains to the reading curriculum and that its print does not warrant any particular attention on account of the demands it makes upon readers. Many of the reading skills demanded by both paper and electronic print are common to both, but there is considerable subjective data and a growing body of empirical research to suggest that there are significant differences between the two media as presenters of print. These differences might be such that they debilitate the transfer of skills between the media. We cannot assume that effective book readers will become effective video screen readers. Nor can we trust that pupils exposed to electronic print programs necessarily gain skills that they are willing or able to employ on conventional print. Further, there are idiosyncrasies implicit in the nature of electronic data storage, manipulation and presentation that call upon readers to adopt an expanded concept of the nature of printed matter and then to employ new literacy skills if they are to take full advantage of the medium.

This latter point is crucial. Teachers may choose not to employ computers in their current reading curricula. Their reasons might vary from the pedagogic to the pragmatic, all of them reasonable and cogent, but this is only part of the argument. The issue is not simply the introduction of a new technology to enrich existing practices; it is also a challenge to teachers to enlarge the scope of their present reading curricula. Today's pupils might not gain familiarisation with electronic print in their classrooms but, outside school, they are likely to be confronted with increasing demands made upon them as users of a video screen. All the new media – microcomputer, teletext and video disk – make heavy use of verbally encoded material. At home and at work, the populations of the western world will be invited to use electronic communication systems that will assert the importance of the written word. Unless teachers can be confident their pupils are literate in the new media they will be failing them. Teachers need to be sure that pupils can summon print to appear on a visual display unit and that they can read it once displayed. If children can do this direct from the written page, all well and good; but if the curriculum needs extension to accommodate new media and new skills, teachers must act upon the imperative.

Legibility (1): viewing conditions

Let us begin by considering the question of legibility. In any medium this is a difficult subject to analyse – not least because so much depends not on the medium alone but on each particular reader and on the degree and nature of that reader's interaction with the medium. Any attempt to consider the legibility of electronic print is fraught with problems. Here, the investigator is dealing with a medium that is highly 'interactive', where so much depends upon user response. To take an example of this in practice, many teachers can often be heard to criticise video displays for their poor legibility and programs for their trouble-some readability. Pupils, on the other hand, are not necessarily affected by the assumed limitations of either hardware or software. Motivated by the medium itself, young readers often cope with text that their teachers consider beyond their resources.

I know of one parent who is convinced that her son was so determined to master this new medium that he taught himself to read via the on-screen prompts of the games software he had been bought for his new computer. The computer he had been given was a low budget model, often criticised by adults for the poor quality of its print output. The text he read consisted of the usual terse, ungrammatical and sometimes obscure captions so characteristic of much commercial software. In his particular case, the medium offered far more than many of us thought it denied.

Viewing conditions constitute one set of variables pertinent to legibility. Incorrect setting of colour, contrast or brightness are beyond the control of the hardware or software manufacturer, yet it is important that users be encouraged to note and adjust them if necessary. It seems that many teachers do not pay attention to such matters in day-to-day computer utilisation in the classroom. Even when buying a screen on which to display their software, these considerations are often secondary to them. Most teachers responsible for the purchase of computer hardware are not primarily concerned with its use for language teaching, nor even for the display of text. Teachers of computer programming are more likely to be concerned with the specifications of the central processing unit, size of memory and so on than they are with the actual display – even when it is going to be used to display program listings on screen. Often they will manage to find enough money to buy a computer but only afterwards will they give any thought to a monitor, buying whatever they can then afford with what little money they have left. Teachers of language arts are in the same economic situation if they want to implement the new technology. The computer is standard, but they can cut the cost on a display screen.

Some teachers will wish for a second or larger display screen. Again it is easy to pay scant regard to the quality of the display, making do with cheap second-hand RF receivers no longer used by their first owners for broadcast reception. It is not difficult to see why these television sets were discarded when one attempts to read the screen. The cathode ray tube has often passed its prime and the controls have deteriorated to an extent where they can no longer offer the fine tuning required to make the screen display acceptable to readers. In choosing a suitable screen for text, the cathode ray tube must be of high quality and the controls still capable of fine adjustment. Further, a video monitor rather than a conventional RF television set is really demanded by the situation, and if a colour monitor can be afforded so much the better. These require-ments make the hardware more expensive but they enhance viewing, reduce physical discomfort and provide more potential than screens that do not comply with these requirements.

Given a good quality video monitor and a correct setting of screen controls, there are still other factors at play for the reader, factors less relevant or even inapplicable to the page of printed text. The viewing angle of the screen is critical; a prevalent recommendation is that viewers should not be at an angle of less than 30 degrees to the plane of the screen. Distance is a reiated factor. Now that computers are interfaced to video screens, viewers are encouraged to sit far closer to the screen than in the past. The reasons are part practical, part psychological. Computers require active rather than passive watching of the screen and the degree of interaction draws the user into a close and sometimes private or even intimate relationship with the technology. Secondly, the mechanics of interfacing are still governed by short cables and proximity to shared power points. Only recently have some hardware manufacturers contemplated wireless infra red and other remote means of communication between home computer and screen. At the same time, however, some developers are drawing users even nearer to the screen.

My own young daughter frequently approaches the screen to point out, or simply explore in a tactile way, part of the display that has attracted her attention. Touch-sensitive screens encourage all users to develop the habits. This is a little worrying. Let alone the fact that colour television sets emit an amount of radiation, most researchers still recommend that the optimum distance from a screen for satisfactory viewing is somwhere between 3 and 12 times the width of the set. Of course much will depend on the exact content of the display. Most viewers will need to sit closer to a screen if they are reading text rather than watching a still or moving image, especially if that image is in close-up. It is important that readers of the screen are aware of the situation and choose appropriate individual positions from which to view. This ought even to involve a willingness to adjust position or furniture according to the particular use to which viewers are going to put the versatile video screen from one moment to the next. Considering the passivity of many viewers of broadcast television – to the extent where inertia precludes even a change of channel between broadcasts – educators have a considerable challenge on their hands.

Movement of the furniture is not quite so drastic, nor so frivolous, as it might seem. It often becomes necessary just to see the screen display at all. Video images are light emitting and may be easily obscured by direct or bright ambient light. Such sources of light need therefore to be closed off, either at source or by moving the screen to a suitably shaded position. As technology advances, cathode ray display mechanisms will become more lightweight and compact. Viewers should be encouraged to adapt their viewing conditions to suit, both now and in preparation for the flat screen and truly portable electronic print display mechanisms of the future. Before long, we will have electronic devices based upon other display principles. We already have limited display power in plasma and liquid crystal devices. These forms of display reduce the problems of perception in that, like conventional printed pages, they depend on reflected rather than emitted light. But as long as we continue to rely on the cathode ray tube we will continue to need an awareness of the importance of viewing conditions. Certainly in the early stages of the electronic society developing around us, an awareness of these conditions and an ability to control them will be part of the skills required for efficient reading of an electronic screen.

Legibility (2): print characters

We may classify viewing conditions as external factors in screen legibility. They are concerned with the display medium and its situation rather than with the microprocessor itself. Beyond them, there lies a set of internal variables governing the legibility of electronic print. These divide into two categories: firstly factors dealing with the characteristics of the generated printed symbols themselves – typeface, size of fount, leading, stroke width, length of line and so on; secondly, factors dealing with the characteristics of the background – colour, resolution, brightness and contrast. (In the latter case it is important to distinguish between those factors determined by the hardware and software manufacturers on the one hand, and those determined by the user, who sets up the controls of the screen, on the other.)

To begin with the first category, electronic print is displayed in dot matrices, which may appear unfamiliar to many users. This is not the only way in which characters are generated but it is the most common on microcomputers used in the home and school. Briefly, each character space on the screen consists of a grid of squares or points, some of which are blocked in to form the character. The size of the dot matrix varies considerably and may generally consist of anything from 10×8 to 9×5 locations. With all of them, some of the finer detail of typical print character sets must be sacrificed on the screen, and compromises must be effected in the drawing of each letter. Readers are likely to find that some character shapes appear distinctly unfamiliar. In other cases, the constraints remove important clues towards individual letter perception or group letter differentiation.

In a typical dot matrix of 7×9 dot locations some alphanumeric symbols are frequently confused. *Z* and *2*, *B* and *8*, and *G* and *C* are notorious examples. Such dot matrices enforce a supression of both ascenders and descenders on lower-case characters despite the fact that these provide important clues for readers. In an attempt to give more prominence to these features, some microcomputers generate lower-case character that do not 'sit' on the base line. Rather they rise above it to allow for a longer descender to be shown. In such cases, however, the text loses its uniformity, word shape is distorted and the descenders are transmuted to simple downstrokes. Some microcomputers still do not even offer any form of lower-case character set. This fact is likely to increase further the problems of letter and word perception and differentiation.

Even when computers do permit the use of lower-case characters, some machines can be called upon to do so only via difficult commands. In my early programming days on an American computer, it took me many weeks to discover how to generate lower-case text from the computer on which I was working. At first, I did not even realise the computer could produce lower case, though this last fact was as much my ignorance of computing as it was the fault of machine design or manufacturer's documentation. There is no encouragement here for teachers who, eager though they are to devise or modify computer software, will not have the time or the expertise to explore the hidden memory recesses of their own particular machine. There is also no inducement for the more advanced programmer if lower-case characters are difficult to command, expensive in terms of the memory they take up or inelegant in program coding. Such constraints really ought not to be tolerated on microcomputers designed for the domestic or educational markets.

In early generations of microcomputers, the programmer or user had to accept whatever typeface or fount the machine offered. The only alternative was to change machine. This was an expensive and impractical option. In any case, there was little to choose between the textual displays of competing computer manufacturers. Later models of micro-computer have improved the situation. To begin with, some micro-computers afford a choice of founts. One of the most popular computers currently used in British schools offers eight different display modes for high and low resolution graphics and text. One of these modes offers the standard teletext character set, while the others offer a range of founts and a choice of 20, 40 or 80 characters to the line. Aspect ratio is an important factor in print legibility, so this is a versatile facility on offer. Unfortunately, it must be added that 20 characters per line are insufficient for continuous text. They cause multitudinous enjambments and space redundancies that add to the eye fatigue resulting from continuous, rapid eye oscillation across short lines of text. On the other hand, an 80-character line is ill-defined on conventional RF receivers and requires a high definition video monitor for easy viewing.

Perhaps a more significant characteristic of the newer microcomputers is a facility for re-defining the shape of individual characters. This comes into its own in software designed for foreign language teaching where there are often idiosyncratic typographic and diacritic features of characters to be displayed. For readers of English, it also permits the operation of reader or teacher preference for founts in terms of their legibility or their use to meet a specific set of perceived educational needs. Two of the machines currently recommended for use in British schools offer the programmer an opportunity to modify the dot matrices of characters. At the moment, this re-definition can be a little complex but there is no reason why software could not present an initial routine whereby teachers could be allowed to re-define characters under program control. Simpler still, users would be allowed to select, from a proffered menu at the outset of a program, a particular fount for the text they will encounter. An alternative approach might offer more versatility if it could be developed beyond its present state.

Character generation programs are already available for some micro-computers. A typical example prints a grid on which a cursor can be moved. Simple depression of one of two keys will place a dot in position under the cursor. The other key will remove any dot that has already been placed. Two further keys are available: one for erasing the whole grid and one for saving the re-drawn character. In this way, a maximum of ten characters can be saved on tape or disk for future use. From such a program, one can foresee software allowing teachers or pupils to define their own character sets, save them and then load them into the computer before loading in the main program to be worked on. If a more permanent modification of the character set is required, it is already possible to define your own character set in this way and then send the cassette or disk off to a specialist service that will blow a new EPROM (Erasable Programmable Read Only Memory) chip containing the newly defined characters. This chip is then substituted for the normal character generator ROM (Read Only Memory) chip in your computer.

It is not too fanciful to suggest that computer users may soon have access to a range of founts. Teachers or pupils might be able to select from one of a predetermined range of textual modes provided by the hardware or to define more specifically individual characters they wish to use. If the number of redefined characters available can be enlarged, this will increase a teacher's access to a range of founts to suit pedagogic beliefs, the abilities of pupils and the teacher's objectives in teaching them. If teachers so wish, they will be able to approximate more closely the fount familiar to their pupils from the books they have been reading. Alternatively, teachers may wish to develop readers' ability to decode not only progressively smaller print but also a wide range of typefaces both familiar and unfamiliar.

Print size and spacing are two further features of legibility. Most visual display units present textual frames of 24 or 25 lines of text with spacing between and a considerable top and bottom border. It is possible that this may contribute to illegibility, for it has been recommended by at least one authority[7] that minimum lettering size should be at the very least $1/25$ picture height and more appropriately $1/10$. According to these standards, all current computer displayed symbols are too small. Even the double-height characters available in teletext displays are less than $1/10$. The size of print might contribute to some pupils' difficulty in decoding even lower-case electronic print. Tinker[8] has shown that upper-case type has the advantage of being seen more easily from a distance and thus suffers less from being smaller if a reader is in close proximity to a screen. Lower-case letters give more clues for decoding but only if seen at closer proximity or if they are larger.

In terms of the spacing between lines, that on most visual displays accords well with many findings, which suggest that the optimum should be ½ to 1 times the height of the symbols. If it is less, it could cause eye fatigue, so a programmer ought to consider writing text on alternate lines. Here, though, if the spacing is too wide, eye movement will be inefficient. Readers of present-day video displays must already contend with a short line pattern that interrupts the natural pattern of eye movements. Further inhibition and confusion might result from narrow line spacing or even from the varying display of well-spaced program captions interspersed with the direct machine messages to a user, which typically appear on consecutive rather than alternate lines.

Narrow line spaces can destroy the visual cohesion of a text: if the space between words is larger than that between consecutive lines of text, the eye tends to be drawn towards a vertical rather than horizontal alignment, and this can be distracting if not disconcerting for a less fluent reader.

Horizontal spacing between words is dependent upon the print statements in each program and can easily conform to the ½ to 1 symbol width, which seems to be appropriate. Similar criteria apply to the 2 to 3 symbol widths advocated between sentences. More difficult is the spacing between letters, since proportional spacing is not yet commonly available on microcomputers. No matter what the width of each character, the same amount of space is allotted to its display. Characters that are fully rounded appear crowded together while letters consisting of a few downstrokes (like *l*) appear isolated in such letter groupings. The unevenly textured print that this creates can be offputting, especially where it creates strong vertical columns of space running through the text. Letter spacing can be varied on machines where characters can be re-defined to give a wider border to the dot matrix, but the process is time-consuming and only partially successful even where it is available.

Legibility (3): screen background

The second set of legibility factors referred to above concerned not so much the characters themselves but their background and their relationship with it. Harrison and Braverman[9] have concluded that black characters on a white background appear to be the most legible. One can postulate that this might be due in no small measure to the conventions that readers bring with them from book to screen. If this is so, it is not clear that the same criterion would apply to beginner readers.

A white screen background consists of direct rather than reflected light as on the page. Physiologically, this might mitigate any psychological preference for such a background colour. Now that many computers have a range of many colours, a more pertinent factor is chromaticity versus achromaticity. With the introduction of new keyboards into BASIC dialects, programmers are able to define the colour of Paper, Border and Ink if they so wish. Recent research into teletext displays has concluded that one of the most acceptable colour combinations is blue or red on white followed by white or yellow on black. Certain colour combinations are virtually illegible: magenta on red, cyan on green or white on yellow. For highlighting in teletext, coloured type is better than coloured background. As an alternative, upper case may be used – except that upper case is read less efficiently than lower case.

It would be wrong to advocate a slavish adherence to these recommendations. Legibility is, after all, a difficult concept in which size, spacing, type fount, contrast and chromaticity all interact with viewing conditions, reader motivation, preference, past experience and familiarity to produce a legibility continuum. Combinations of several factors, each of which has only a slight influence on relative legibility, can produce significantly lower legibility. Added to this must be the aims and objectives of each teacher. There may be occasions when optimal legibility is expressly not required, when the aim is specifically to present a reader with less preferentially legible text; in this way it is hoped that the reader will extend his ability to decode less familiar text.

Some of the research is likely to produce standards for software and hardware designers. Where this is the case teachers should take note of the conditions and prepare their pupils to cope with the print demands of the medium. Take teletext, for example. There is already evidence from junior schools[10] that some readers are daunted by the uniform solid blocks of text and by the unfamiliar computer forms of certain letters. But there are, and there will continue to be, other founts on the screen and on paper with which readers must contend.

Perhaps more than anything else, teachers of reading must equip their pupils with the confidence and versatility to cope with the current diversity of texts and print media and to adjust to the future rapid changes that are likely to be the result of technological advance. In this respect it is important to remember just how large a part the electronic medium might play as a future print medium. It is no accident that words like Paper, Border and Ink found their way into BASIC programming dialects as soon as colour became available for programmers to use. Nor is it coincidental that information is stored on video disk in chapters, data on floppy disk or tape as files. This electronic medium is the natural successor to the Gutenberg press. If anything, its advent is likely to increase rather than decrease the demand for literacy. In meeting that demand, computers can be powerful reading aids. Whether they are to be used to foster current reading skills or to familiarise readers with a print medium of the future, computers offer teachers a novel, large, yet also simple, manipulable and versatile medium for the display of a diversity of print formats.

Comprehension

The decoding of legible characters is an aimless activity unless it is accompanied by the acquisition of some meaning. This shifts the focus away from the text itself towards readers' response to what they read, and this response or understanding can be registered by a computer. More than that, a computer is able to act upon the response in a truly interactive way.

Many early computer programs were of the simplest form of comprehension exercise. Computers were seen as a replication of classroom activity rather than as an extension of it. Often, the reading curriculum culminated in the reading of literature on the one hand and in the comprehension exercise on the other. These comprehension exercises consisted of short extracts for reading followed by a set of questions designed to test literal and inferential understanding of the test. Sometimes readers were also asked to make an evaluative response to the content or style of the passage. These activities could be easily implemented on a computer. The presentation of short passages of text singled out from their context well evaded the problems of limited electronic storage and display of text. The problem of computer acceptance and interpretation of response to questioning could easily be overcome by the use of multiple choice menus from which to select an answer.

Today, these comprehension activities have been largely discredited – in ordinary classroom activity away from a computer at least. They have been replaced by other reading strategies designed by teachers to create greater involvement with a text and to elucidate meaning. Microcomputers are still able to replicate these more recent teaching strategies. Moreover, the computer affords new reading experiences for pupils: some children might accept the new medium but not conventional print. All of them stand to gain from exposure to print in a variety of contexts and from familiarity with an increasingly important print medium. In addition, the teacher is released for other tasks in the classroom. As well as providing these opportunities, the computer can extend the comprehension activities of readers.

'Cloze' and other deletion programs

One of the reading strategies common today is 'cloze' procedure. In this activity, readers are presented with a text in which words have been deleted at a regular interval of, say, every seventh word. Using any syntactic or semantic clues they perceive, readers then try to replace the missing words and so complete the text. There are on the market a number of cloze procedure programs. They were quick to appear as soon as programmers began to consider what software they could produce exploiting the computer's power to manipulate language in structure and visual form. In the version I have developed for use with pupils, the frequency of word omission can be changed each time any text is displayed.

An important reservation is necessary about the implementation of cloze procedure on a computer. In classrooms, it is nearly always a group activity. The task is not to reconstitute the text the author created. Rather the goal is to produce an acceptable text cohering in content, grammar and style. Pupils often propose several alternative words. The value of the exercise lies in the animated group discussion of which alternative to adopt. Pupil versions may vary considerably from the original, and teachers who have used this reading activity value pupil discussion of the differences between the two and their justification of their own version (which may be superior). When the activity is managed by a computer, the activity loses much of its purpose. Sometimes pupils work on their own against the computer. Too often they are encouraged simply to identify the missing words. This places the emphasis on correctness rather than on originality. In some versions, pupils are given the writer's original word after three 'unsuccessful' attempts at finding the original. In one version they are given clues concerning the number of letters constituting the word; in another, they are helped by being told if and where, by chance, they might have placed a correct letter even if the word itself is 'wrong' (that is, by comparison with the original). The total benefit of the activity is not always lost: I have known a heated discussion when pupils choose a perfectly acceptable word that is not accepted by the computer. The exchanges become very animated – especially when the eventual revelation of the original text shows a far less interesting use of words than that of the pupils.

The computer is certainly good at manipulating text, but we should not expect too much of it. Once a text is in a computer, a cloze procedure program need go no further than processing and displaying it on screen or as hard copy. It would be possible for the machine to prepare a number of versions of the same text, each with a different frequency of deletion. This would be ideally suitable to readers of disparate ability (the number of deletions increasing in direct proportion to the ability of the reader). Some interesting discussion will also arise following the use of a number of different versions all being used by equally able readers. If a visual display unit rather than a printout is used for the presentation and completion of the text, then it should accept any user input rather than attempt to match it to the original. At the end, the screen could be split to provide the original and new versions of the text side by side for comparison and discussion. A printout of both versions could also be provided. This would give the added advantage of a permanent record of the user version, which could later be compared with the versions of the same text completed by other users.

Whereas cloze procedure programs are based on the idea of partial deletion, there are now a number of programs based on total deletion. In these, all words are deleted, leaving only information about word divisions and punctuation. Users are challenged to reconstruct the text by replacing individual letters or complete words in the text. In some versions, all the letters are replaced by asterisks. In a version that I have developed, readers can be challenged further. Deleted text can be replaced by asterisks but users can also opt for a total absence of any markers locating the text. They can also remove the punctuation if they are feeling particularly adventurous. Thus, users are faced with a blank page on which there may be some clues or none. The text then begins to emerge from this void and take shape on the screen. Readers are asked to employ a large number of reading skills and pick up many clues to complete the text. A scoring system is built in so that readers are encouraged to adopt efficient strategies for reconstituting the page of text. The skills employed range from elementary perceptual decoding skills to semantic comprehension. Some versions of this type of software make reading for meaning more explicit. One program offers a question and then asks the reader to constitute and assimilate only as much text as is necessary to answer the question.

Sequencing and ordering

There are other reading programs that also exploit the combined computer features of dynamic display, rapid data manipulation and interactivity. Sequencing is a further strategy increasingly employed by teachers. Pupils are given jumbled sentences or larger units of language to arrange into a meaningful discourse. Computers are very efficient at rearranging language in this way; it is one of the major attributes of a word processor.

A number of programs are available. Some begin with word sequencing of sentences before graduating to nursery rhymes and prose paragraphs. In theory, there is no reason why a computer cannot present larger units of text to order. In practice, the issue is complicated by the display limitations of the screen. With only 24 or 25 lines of text visible at any one time, the constant scanning to and fro over a number of paragraphs becomes cumbersome if the screen must be constantly scrolled or if two or three static frames of text have frequently to be re-called. A single screen of text holds fewer paragraphs than a page of print. It can hold far less than a table-top spread with slips of cut-up paper, each with a paragraph on it, which is the way most teachers present sequencing. The larger the units of text to be ordered, the more cumbersome the computer display and the more varied and potentially confusing the ocular and manual skills demanded in summoning, reading and re-arranging the textual units.

There might be some positive good to be gained here. Despite the problems, computers are likely to be used for the display of large units of text beyond the classroom. Readers will need to develop perceptual, manual and cognitive skills to move efficiently through a text from one screen to the next. Perhaps this type of software could help them overcome, or at least become aware of, the problems of memory and manual dexterity involved in moving between frames or scrolling through text where only small fragments of the work may be visible at any one time. For the most part, however, sequencing activities on a computer are best confined to small, self-contained units of text. Here the problems are not evident and programmers are free to use the computer to favourable advantage. They can use its randomising feature to present the text in ever-varying orders. They can also use its ability to match user input with original.

One ingenious suite of programs is a compendium of three games based on three different principles of re-ordering, which taken together offer considerable practice at all levels of written English structure. The first program selects a text from a data file and then proceeds to isolate at random a word within that text. The chosen word is then anagrammed and replaced for the reader to identify and spell correctly. The second program adopts a similar format but this time it scrambles a series of words within a chosen text. The final program selects a whole text, randomly re-ordering each sentence within it and then numbering them in a scrambled version for subsequent re-ordering.

There is always the danger in these programs that language software may become so prescriptive that it precludes originality. Sentences can often be restructured in a totally different way without changing the meaning. The same is just as true of other units of language. Sometimes, a restructuring can be a distinct improvement. The re-arrangement can also make subtle re-emphases to the meaning of the utterance, but this can be acceptable even within the context of the surrounding argument. Software ought to facilitate rather than restrict language use. Specific software can generate countless random organisations of language for sequencing activities, but its usefulness may be questioned if readers are asked only to establish the original textual sequence. A word processor is so much more useful: teachers can key in texts and re-arrange them on screen; they can then print out as worksheets a large variety of jumbled sequences. Alternatively, these jumbled versions can then be saved on tape or disk for later use by pupils. They re-arrange them on screen and then save or print out their versions. These results can be later compared with the original or with the versions of peers. In terms of visual presentation, there will be no marked difference between the original and the pupil versions to intrude upon any comparative evaluation. All copies will appear typographically similar and of equal eminence. Attention will be focused on the content of the language alone.

Prediction

Prediction is another technique that could make use of the computer's ability to manipulate strings of textual characters and provide interaction with users in a structured way. As employed in class, pupils are presented with short passages of text. After reading each, they are guided in discussion (possibly via question and answer) towards predict-ing how the narrative will continue; and they are expected to make use of all the syntactic and semantic clues in the text.

On a computer, frames of text could be displayed with multiple choice selections stating various further developments. After keying in a choice corresponding to the actual narrative flow, the computer could respond by presenting the subsequent part of the narrative. if the choice is at variance with the narrative, the program could present frames of advice or respond to a mistaken choice by re-directing readers to a very specific part of the narrative for them to re-read before making their choice again. A more imaginative approach would be to allow readers to follow the course of their predictions.

Computers will soon be able to summon any of a vast number of frames of text at lightning speed. There could be any number of narratives available, and readers could be allowed to follow their predictions to a conclusion. That might result in the termination of the narrative (possibly with the opportunity of returning to the point of deviation for a second chance); a reconnection with the narrative at a later point; or a looping back to an earlier part (to show readers how they have misread an incident). A computer could structure and manage prediction tasks in a far more rigorous way than the teacher, particularly where there may be several small groups working together in the classroom. The computer can conceal and reveal text at exactly the right moment, and efficiently direct users to retrieve whichever passage of text is immediately appropriate.

Higher reading skills

As reading progresses, emphasis shifts from individual and small clusters of symbols to larger sequences of connected words, phrases and sentences. As we have already seen, however, the larger the textual unit, the more problematic its display on a computer.

Line length and spacing for reading fluency

Our eyes move over print in a regular halting rhythm, stopping periodically along each line to fixate and take in a section of text. The optimum line length for conventional print has been shown to be between 50 and 60 characters per line. Yet shorter lines are the norm on most microcomputers. A 40-column screen has become the standard, though some computers present as few as 22 columns. Anything more than 40 columns is likely to impair legibility especially where text is presented on the inferior display of a conventional television set rather than on a video monitor. On the other hand, only 40 columns or less will interrupt the regular fixations readers make as their eyes move over the text.

Spacing between lines will also be important for fluent reading of the screen. Unfortunately, line spacing is predetermined and inflexible on a visual display unit. Extreme care must be taken here with the use of sequential lines of text in block capitals. Texts written entirely in upper case will appear uniformly dense and daunting. In extreme cases the letters may even appear to fuse. If line spacing is less than word spacing then the visual cohesion of the text will appear to be vertical rather than horizontal and the lines will be less easy to follow. Close line spacing also makes it difficult for the eyes to make accurate return sweeps to following lines.

Texts written on alternate lines can also present problems: too much space again makes for inefficient eye movement; it will also spread the text out beyond the confines of a single frame and require a dynamic rather than static form of display. This will bring with it further motor and cognitive demands as users manipulate the text on screen and follow on an argument or narrative over a repeatedly replenished screen.

Display formats as learning prompts

Serious attention needs to be paid to the dynamic presentation of text on electronic screens. For a beginning reader, it is important that letter display follows a left-to-right sequence with captions appearing visibly a letter or word at a time – rather in the way that print appears from an electric typewriter or uni-directional computer printer. At higher reading levels, the eyes do not move smoothly at an even rate from left to right across each letter but rather in short fixations across the text. At each fixation readers take in only as many visual cues as they need to decode and assimilate the text. It would be inappropriate to enforce the inefficient eye movement of early readers on more fluent readers of the screen. For them it is better to reveal the whole caption at once (as a computer can deceive the eye into believing). Users' eyes can then make their own halting, saccadic movements over the text, each user determining his or her own fixations and eye spans.

This textual redundancy is not confined to letters alone but works also at higher levels of syntax, increasing as a reader grows in proficiency. Once readers have mastered particular structural features of language and know their meaning when they read them, they will not linger over every word but become more likely to fixate on only the more important words rather than prepositions, articles, conjunctions, verbal auxiliaries and so on. Here there might be a very specific argument for the re-introduction of dynamic textual presentation and for the use of some overt instruction programs.

I have always found it difficult to foster among children some of the higher order skills like speed reading and scanning. Some teachers and parents never do provide tuition beyond this point. Once children have learned the elementary decoding and comprehension skills, it is often assumed they have learned to read, and they are left to fend for themselves. They have little more to learn, it is said, other than what can be gained from further practice. Too often the reading curriculum stops here and turns into a course in literary criticism. If, on the other hand, we believe that readers still have many skills to learn beyond early reading competence, then computers may certainly offer teaching opportunities that have been unknown or ineffectual hitherto.

Computers are limited in the extent to which they can employ many of the graphic opportunities available to conventional typographers. Electronic print cannot afford many of the typographic clues that readers normally make use of. Instead, some new typographic conventions are appearing to replace these conventional 'signposts'. One of the most obvious is the different colouring of each paragraph in a frame of text to distinguish between them. Often this replaces the use of indentation or line spacing as paragraph markers, because space is at a premium in an electronic frame of text. If we are thinking of overt reading programs, then the use of upper case, coloured text or background and animated display in real time can emphasise particular language structures or encourage particular eye movements.

A program could prompt appropriate eye fixations through the way text is presented on the screen. The rapid presentation of many phrase, clause and sentence structures of the same type would encourage the eyes to fixate on the new item in each group while peripheral vision assimilated the rest of the structure. Perhaps beginning with verb and prepositional phrases, graded activities could progress to simple nouns phrases, short relative clauses and so on. Reinforcement could be applied by the use of coloured text to highlight salient key words in sentences or (later) topic sentences in paragraphs, thus encouraging readers to ignore the less important, if not semantically redundant, features of a text. Both the amount of text displayed in each frame and the time permitted for each display could be increased so that the activity evolved into a speed reading process. This is one of the ultimate higher order reading skills and an essential one given the rate of display of so much electronic text today.

Studies of good readers have shown that they tend to have more regular eye movements, shorter fixations, wider eye spans and fewer regressions than other readers. Some attempts have been made to develop resources to cultivate these attributes. The tachistoscope was a machine which projected whole groups of words on to a screen for a pre-set time so that readers were encouraged to perceive the whole word group at one fixation. By reducing the time gap between each exposure, the intention was to reduce the length of time between each fixation during reading. Such brief projections are a simple matter for a computer-controlled video display. Not only can a computer regulate the activity precisely via its internal clock; it can also monitor reader assimilation and respond accordingly. Each individual exposure or series of exposures can be followed by a comprehension question, the answer to which the computer monitors before repeating the task or proceeding at a faster or slower exposure rate as appropriate.

The pacer was another mechanism invented to develop speed reading skills. It was a mechanical device that moved a shutter at a pre-set speed over a page of print to eliminate re-reading and regression. The limited portion of a whole text available in any one frame of a computer display already confronts readers with this situation. The format can be further developed as an explicit learning activity through the use of a dynamic display of text on screen. A number of different display formats could be adopted. In a static frame of text, sections could be blacked or highlighted in turn. Successive screens of text could be replenished via scrolling or whole frame replacement – in both cases, readers being discouraged or debarred from returning to earlier sections of the text.

Contextualised reading skills

As so often with reading strategies, it is important here not to forget that reading is far more than a technical activity. Strategies for the development of specific reading techniques can prove attractive to pupils if they are embodied in a game. Besides the fun element of such software, it is also more likely that the activity will be given some purpose even if it is only to obtain a higher score. But reading itself has a purpose. Its immediate function is to extract meaning from the printed symbols, yet this comprehension is often part of a wider purpose that caused the reader to access a text in the first place. Good software will recognise this and attempt to incorporate reading activities in a functional context.

One speed reading program, which recognises the entertainment value of software and the semantic function of reading, displays a simple table of facts on screen while a randomly generated sentence 'ribbons' past below the table. If the sentence is true according to the facts in the table, the sentence must be trapped on screen by the depression of a single key. Points are scored for correctness and speed of response. One of my skim reading programs presents readers with static frames of text to skim and so sets out to encourage rapid eye movements over the text. Slow readers are helped by the use of on-screen highlighting of important key words and topic sentences if they fail to move on after a pre-specified time limit. The highlighting begins at the top of the screen and proceeds from left to right across each line in a further attempt to encourage efficient eye movements. After each frame of text, there is a series of multiple choice questions and answers to test literal, inferential and evaluative comprehension of the text.

An important advantage of this program is that it is accompanied by a utility program allowing teachers to input and save their own texts. These can consist of individual or multiple frames of print. They may be purely verbal but may also include graphics. Thus annotated illustrations and teletext frames combining text and graphics are possible as textual resources for speed reading. More than this, the intention is to allow teachers or pupils to build up a large store of print data so that readers may exercise higher order skills in a more meaningful context. This is important, for the speed of reading will depend to a large extent not only on the fluency of a reader but also on the text itself and the reader's reasons for referring to it. The ideal situation would be to create a number of electronic frames of text relevant to other classroom resources and the activity in hand. It might be that the computer stores the transposition of a conventional book or some totally new information that pupils may wish to access as they would other reference materials. They can then approach the computer to gain the information required while at the same time be encouraged or required to use higher order reading strategies.

Interactive reading strategies

Speed reading is not the only form of higher reading skill. Efficient readers are not necessarily just skilled in speed reading, but can also adopt a variety of reading strategies to suit the material and circumstances and their objectives in reading it. In the past it might have been said that television, the electronic medium most widely available, presented only a very limited amount of continuous text and that even that was of little linguistic diversity. Such criticisms are not relevant to the new electronic technology. Certainly, the storage of verbal text is expensive in terms of memory but improvements are taking place. A video disk when interfaced with a computer can offer at least 46,000 frames of electronic print. Microcomputers can also be linked to central data bases.

British Telecom's Prestel, a viewdata service available via a computer linked to the telephone network, is a good example of such text storage facilities. It demonstrates that we are no longer talking hypothetically, nor are we considering only an educational resource. Prestel is a commercial reality with a growing number of personal and public subscribers. The existence of such electronic data communication systems raise questions about future literacy to which we must return. At the moment, Prestel offers over 300,000 frames of text, though there is 'virtually no limit to the number of pages of information available to the user'. Teletext, too, offers a substantial quantity of electronic print material. Between them, the teletext services of all the British television channels offer many hundred pages of text. If more frequencies become available with the closure of some of the old frequency transmission services or with the introduction of cable relay, it has been suggested that the way could be open for a dedicated teletext channel carrying over 50,000 pages. At the same time, Fedida and Malik, pioneers of the British viewdata system, expect that 'the immediate limitation arising from the existing screen technology . . . will eventually change as the receivers are expanded to 80 characters a line, which is likely to happen in the mid-eighties'.[11]

This forecast is obviously precipitate, but it seems reasonable to assume that large quantities of text will soon be commercially available upon which readers can exercise their skill; or rather, skills, since the interactive nature of this new technology both permits and demands the exercise of a variety of reading skills. Broadcast television could have been criticised for its inducement towards one rapid, sequential reading strategy. The pace was determined by producer, not reader, and the rate of display was fast in the interests of economy or sheer slickness of presentation. It rarely altered; and, being a broadcast system, the rate of display tended towards the lowest common denominator acceptable to a mass audience. Even educational reading programmes were unable to regulate their delivery to suit individual requirements. To some extent, the invention of the domestic video tape recorder allowed more viewer control of pace but the display was still sequential to all intents and purposes. Now the video disk and floppy disk allow rapid random access to frames of text with the ability to hold each frame indefinitely. Teletext offers similar facilities in a very structured way through its paging system. (Access time will continue to be slow until the service is available as a dedicated channel or via cable, as it is with the British Prestel service.) Regression, re-reading, skimming, scanning and searching were all limited or impossible via television before the advent of interactive technology. Now readers not only can, but must, make use of these reading strategies if they are to benefit from the electronic print resources being made available to them.

We should not underestimate the degree of sophisticated high order reading skills that computers seem to demand even when we are not embodying these skills in teaching software. Electronic print displays will put a premium upon speedy and efficient comprehension. Sometimes, individual words and phrases appear anywhere on screen in exposures of brief duration. Sometimes text is delivered to screen letter by letter or line by line at a pre-set rate, successive lines of text frequently scrolling off the top of the screen. At other times whole frames of text are exposed and then replaced by others at short pre-set time intervals. Readers must learn to adopt the speed reading skills demanded by the situation. Even where the presentation of text is sufficiently lengthy, readers may still need encouraging to adopt speed reading techniques. Where visual display screens act as on-line terminals with information transmitted in real time, there will be pressures for diminishing the period of time when the terminal is logged on to a host machine. The situation denies access to other users and may increase the outlay in rental of telephone or other transmission charges. Moreover, even if such conditions do not exist, faster reading is likely to be encouraged by the ephemeral and transitory nature of the medium and the small sections of text presented in any one display frame. The reader is urged to pursue an experience or an argument, not just in the next column, but awaiting on a screen now totally hidden from view. The effect produced is much like that of the reading improvement machines mentioned earlier in that small units of moving text are presented, pressing the reader on to attain greater and greater speeds of comprehension.

There are a number of high order reading strategies. Proficient readers are those who can adopt a strategy suitable to the text before them and their requirements in reading it. For such readers there are many occasions when they do not assimilate a text in linear fashion. Initially, it is likely that their attention will focus on only the first one or two paragraphs and on the conclusion to the text in an attempt to establish topic, theme or style. Thereafter, readers may decide to read an article in its entirety. Or they may skim the text looking for key words and topic sentences, only occasionally pausing to read discrete units in greater detail. If such text is presented in a computerised form, readers would need to adopt a more overt, active strategy. Because a computer screen can hold only a small number of words at any one time, this must have a profound effect on the nature of the skim reading and of scanning. A newspaper can be scanned and the relevant pieces identified very quickly. If a visual display unit can provide access to some 1,000 characters alone at any one time, the same process has to take much longer. It will also involve altered eye movements and manual motor skills as the keyboard (or some other peripheral device) is activated to frame further portions of text on screen.

The way frames of text are replaced on screen in any software will thus be important to readers. It will be particularly significant in an explicit approach to the teaching of reading. It could be argued that animating text in its delivery to screen rather than presenting static displays frame by frame will encourage certain higher order reading strategies. So scrolling text could be seen to encourage readers to skim quickly through a text, though its role as an inducement towards retrospective glances at the text as well as anticipatory reading may be questioned. Moreover, even scrolling can retard access to the text for a fluent reader and, being a single continuous column of text, it is likely to encourage bi-directional eye movements rather than the multi-directional movements that good readers employ as they peruse the several columns of a newspaper, magazine, poster or other large-format hard-copy print display. Perversely, therefore, there may be a danger that the electronic presentation of large units of text could militate against non-sequential reading strategies. Compared to, say, the body of text revealed on a single sheet of newspaper, the electronic medium imposes an artificial, definitive window on a very small unit of text. Whether this urges readers to focus on every word, or whether it urges them to skim over the material and to replace the text with the next frame, we do not yet know. It would be a different matter if readers could make imaginative use of the medium's idiosyncrasies. There might be positive advantages if appropriate software could be designed and implemented to encourage readers to scroll both vertically and horizontally over large textual displays (in the manner of some of the spreadsheet software currently available), if it gave them access to a number of text windows so they could hold one on screen while calling up another in juxtaposition, or if they could scroll two halves of a screen simultaneously or independently.

Full comprehension of electronic text will thus imply new skills. It is not just a matter of unavoidably quicker reading. Rather it is a case of specific reading strategies like skimming and scanning, of accurate initial perception and longer memory retention. Perhaps some of these skills will be fostered implicitly by the medium if pupils are given frequent access to it. It would be foolish to expect universal acquisition, and poor readers may need structured and explicit mediation by teachers. Even readers expert in accessing and assimilating conventional print may not be optimally proficient in the new medium.

Information retrieval

Microcomputer users need fluent reading skills, but they also need those skills relevant to access and retrieval of electronic data. Not only should they be able to decode with meaning a frame of text; they should also be able to call it up in the first place from a data bank.

Sequential ordering

Some of the access and retrieval skills involved may be traditional. Even these may be learnt via a computer. Since computers can be programmed to perform text handling, data processing and information storage tasks, so their ability to do so can be exploited to explicate and demonstrate on screen in graphic and animated form the strategies involved, and to monitor pupils' ability in employing them against the machine's capacity to do so.

At a simple level, programs to test alphabetical ordering are legion. One of my programs presents a sequence of words in an arbitrary order chosen at random by computer. The user must then sequence each word in turn according to alphabetical order. This same program is used at varying levels from first-letter ordering through to fourth-letter ordering and even higher. It also includes examples for sequential ordering taken from indices (including names, titles and first lines of verse) and from a range of textual sources implying other organisational criteria (gazetteers, directories, dictionaries, encyclopaedias and the contents pages of textbooks). It can be used with another study skills program that encourages readers to scan frames of text from these sources in a rapid but efficient manner in the search for answers to specific questions presented before the text. Readers are then tested on their search and the time is given.

In such instances, a computer need not simply test the reading strategies used; instead, it could actively foster them, re-routing users back to previous frames of text or to the right one when a wrong frame has been accessed. It can be programmed to utilise its graphics capabilities to highlight salient key words, topic sentences or paragraphs and all in carefully monitored and/or controlled real time via its internal clock.

Database access

There are also new skills to be learnt. Precisely because a computer is itself so good at information retrieval and can perform much of the mechanical work traditionally associated with the task, readers can leave much of it to the machine – provided they can command the machine accordingly. So readers need to be conversant in the ways of instructing present information systems and prepared to adapt to those of the future. Pupils should be given the chance to develop these new literate skills. Opportunity should be afforded in school for pupils to engage in work that involves the querying, if not compiling, of data banks using both internal data-storage facilities and those accessed via line terminals.

A large amount of textual data is now publicly available in the form of hierarchical or branching databases. Teletext and viewdata services are of this sort because a tree structure expends fewest computing resources and permits efficient retrieval. To access such a database, users work through a succession of indices, each one refining the subject chosen from the one before until readers are presented with a single frame or series of frames expanding upon the topic of their enquiry. This type of information retrieval has its advantages. It is so highly structured and its method of textual retrieval is so efficient that users can be guided firmly without deviation to the target of their search. For less efficient researchers, this type of database removes the necessity for them to address themselves to the reading of large passages or even whole books of irrelevant information.

At the same time, there are a number of disadvantages. A typical frame of electronic print is a very small window through which to glimpse at a database. Users cannot glance around as in a newspaper, nor flick through the pages as in a book. Browsing can often be an enjoyable experience in itself. It can also be rewarding in that readers sometimes come across unrealised references and source materials of interest to them. Browsing along library shelves or through the pages of a book normally provides readers with a tangible sense of where they are in relation to the rest of the information store. Readers have some idea of the relationship between a page or article in front of them and the rest of the text or texts. With a book or newspaper, then, readers can relate the part to the whole. Electronic information storage and retrieval systems, by contrast, always appear opaque – abstract and intangible in overall form and structure to the information seeker. This could present insurmountable problems for less able users.

As users of an electronic information retrieval system move along its branches, their difficulty in retaining an overall appreciation of the structure of the information before them is likely to be aggravated. Less efficient readers might gain from the direction and example afforded by a tree-structured search of data, but at the same time they can easily be distracted in their search. It is also easy for them to depress the wrong key and summon an inappropriate frame of information. Either way, they can be diverted down an irrelevant branch from which it will be difficult to return unless they are conceptually aware of the structure of the database and the enquiry path they have followed.

Such diversions or mistypings are not confined to the less able. Proficient readers can become just as frustrated working through a long series of frames to elicit the information they require – especially if that information is not available at the end of the pursuit. If the search is successful, good readers might well ask if the information could not have been obtained more efficiently through scanning the same information in a conventional text. Good researchers constantly ask themselves if the information they are currently assimilating is of value to them. If it is not, they will move to another part of the text quickly and efficiently. A branching interaction does not facilitate this strategy.

Really competent users of the medium will wish to make use of its unique search facilities. Computers can provide extremely fast data matching and sorting processes for large amounts of information. The medium is therefore ideal for searches of extensive banks of data using more than one parameter. (For example, in a library catalogue a computer could be commanded to find play titles where AUTHOR = SHAKESPEARE and DATE > 1600.) Hierarchically organised data structures might be most inappropriate for users who wish to retrieve information that has multiple attributes.

Yet another issue is that a branch format ought to be carefully structured to allow it to be mapped on to the cognitive structures or patterns of thought and enquiry of readers. This is an exceedingly difficult task in the first place and, even if the structure of individual cognitive maps does reveal that some hierarchical arrangements are more suitable than others, a database structured in this way is unlikely to be entirely satisfactory for every reader. Alternative ways of representing the information for users need to be considered.

Some hierarchically organised electronic databases have been designed to overcome some of the problems associated with them. One characteristic innovation has been the addition of a search facility in which users can type in key words to gain direct access to a relevant part of the data base. Not only can this cut down access time for an individual page but it can also facilitate jumps from one part of the tree to another. The idea of key words can be taken further in a database comprising simply a collection of individual records. Here the key words could be used to extract individual records and fields from files in a matching process.

New interrogative strategies for information retrieval

A more loosely structured database is likely to satisfy a greater number of reader interactions with the data. Here, however, the language and mode (selective versus generative) of interrogating the information stored might necessitate the acquisition of new reader/user skills, if not concepts. Although this design of information storage and transmission might be potentially very efficient and of new usage, it does rely on the adoption of new literacy strategies that we cannot assume users of electronic print will necessarily develop on their own without teacher intervention. Indeed, electronic databases make considerable cognitive demands upon users.

When information is stored in conventional textbooks and reference manuals, it can often be accessed (though not necessarily assimilated or efficiently extrapolated) using an elementary and singular reading strategy. Many readers do not progress beyond the close reading strategy they first learnt in reading fictional material. They continue to apply this strategy not only to fictional prose but also to reference material whatever their reasons for accessing it. There is no disincentive or overtly preventive measure to stop them doing so. Although it might not be an efficient retrieval strategy, at least these information gatherers are able to access the data.

An electronic database is characteristically not accessible in the same way. The information is stored, retrieved and presented in a form that militates against the superimposition of a linear model on content or application of a close reading strategy, either or both of which readers may try to transfer from their encounter with conventional narrative prose. Users of electronic information retrieval systems have to work hard to summon each frame of information and to relate each to each. If they do not, each screen of information is meaningless – or, worse, the screen remains blank, for users may not know how to retrieve the information they require. The interrogation of a database requires users to formulate hypotheses and embody them in interrogative structures that are compatible with the database structure and system of inter-rogation. Every user of such an information store is thus forced repeatedly to select and adopt the active, self-questioning reading strategies and other cognitive procedures that able readers/researchers adopt whenever they turn to conventional functional print resources.

It is likely that even these conventional reference texts will eventually be stored or composed directly upon computer. Some may be trans-formed entirely to match or maximise upon the stylistic conventions that the new medium now offers and urges upon information providers. But even where the information is provided in a linear textual form, the medium still offers interesting possibilities.

Consider the presentation of conventional texts of a functional nature such as may be found in many subject textbooks. These often com-mence with an abstract followed by a linear argument or analysis. Traditionally, the readers have then to scan the body of text to find the information they require. A computerised version of this resource material could be totally restructured in a branching format to allow readers the choice for divergence at any point of the original synopsis.

They would then be able to follow any particular line of enquiry they wished to pursue. While reading frames of text, an on-screen thesaurus or dictionary could be called upon at any point to elucidate a text meaningless to the reader. Further interrogative features could be built into the programmed text allowing readers to make more interactions with it. These facilities could be summoned through single key strokes or through the keying in of command words during the reading/search process. To summon a dictionary definition, for example, the word 'DEFINE' could be offered. Inputting the word 'ENLARGE' might route readers through a reinforcing loop of the same content material differently expressed or structured. Other forms of graphic presentation could also be available. Keying in the word 'SHOW' could summon a diagrammatic representation of the information embodied in the text.

The implications for education are clear. Pupils must gain familiarity with electronic databases, not just because of their growing importance but also because, designed well and used wisely, electronic databases can foster desirable modes of thinking. Pupils should begin to explore electronic information retrieval systems in a purposeful context where the computer can be seen to be a worthwhile tool for personal enquiry.

Learning programs for schools

There are a number of programs available to introduce users to many of the concepts and skills involved in the establishment and subsequent interrogation of databases. Some are based on the parlour game 'Animal, vegetable or mineral?' Users are asked to think of an object, which the computer then tries to identify in its database via a series of questions. It asks if the object has specific attributes. The answer is a simple 'yes' or 'no', which allows the program to move along a branching tree of information towards the next decision node. If the computer eventually arrives at a wrong identification, users are prompted to input further questions, which the computer will use in later games to distinguish between the items in its database: the tree structure is continually enlarged. Some versions of the game allow users to see on screen a diagrammatic representation of the information tree. Thus users can become more aware of how the information is structured and how the computer operates upon its data.

There are also specific information retrieval systems designed for school use. Examples may be found of all the different generic types of information retrieval systems available. Some are simple and user-friendly since they are designed primarily as introductory familiarisation packages. Others are more extensive in that they are designed as working tools for use in schools. In Britain, the British Library was one of the pioneers producing software to demonstrate the basic principles involved in information storage and retrieval and to provide a practical system that can be used in the classroom to locate teaching and research materials. SIR (Schools Information Retrieval) uses the information retrieval routines from the international database network DIALOG. In trials, the fiction database was used by 11-year-old pupils to learn library and information skills and to prepare them to employ the information system for further project work. This particular database enabled pupils to search for story types appropriate to their age and reading level. Older pupils were able to use the system in the same way but first they had to compile their own database. Examination candidates collected cuttings, read them carefully, selected key words from the articles and entered the information into a microcomputer using the SIR software. The information was then available for retrieval to help them with their chosen examination topic.

When children are given access to electronic information storage and retrieval systems they are not only gaining familiarity with the new skills involved. In order to compile a database, users must be in full command of the subject matter as well as conversant with the proposed means of storing it. In collecting the information from conventional books and other reference sources, pupils can be encouraged to make use of a wide range of reading and study skills. Then in selecting and ordering the material for electronic entry, they will have to structure and categorise it in appropriate and meaningful ways. The cognitive skills involved in the process are considerable while the eventual product can be a valuable resource that can be used by the originators or other pupils to support a range of activities away from the computer. The database can also be employed to give further practice in data compilation through subsequent revision and extension.

As time progresses, more and more public and private databases are opening up. State and commercial communications organisations – telephone companies, broadcasting institutions, newspapers and international news services – are all showing interest in the provision of electronic information facilities for their own and others' use. Some make special provision for school users. Even if not, many databases are readily accessible on-line direct from school premises. We should use them to enrich the resources we make available to children and to provide pupils with valuable experience in the rapidly expanding communications systems that are gaining increasing importance.

The data banks of the future: fact or fiction?

In looking at the quantities of electronic text available, I have been concerned mostly with transactional data and therefore with the functional reading strategies and information retrieval skills primarily associated with it. Since we now have the ability to store and present increasingly larger amounts of electronic textual information, there is no reason why that text should not be narrative fiction as well as transactional prose. Just as there are now central data banks of reference information, fictional texts could also be held in centralised electronic libraries from which users could access particular fictional works on their display screens and even print them out or down-load them at a home terminal for future reference – rather like present tele-software.

Perhaps more likely as computer memory becomes less expensive in terms of storage would be the pre-stored package, be it disk or chip, which could be purchased and accumulated into a personal 'library' of data to be read in conjunction with some form of microprocessor. The video disk is a case in point. Manufacturers are already making an inevitable comparison of the video disk's text storage capacity to that of conventional books. Two video disks can hold more text than the *Encyclopaedia Britannica*. On each disk, data is already stored in 'chapters', thus drawing a parallel with the conventional print medium that the electronic medium could come to rival.

Even the truly portable hand-held silicon book might not be too far in the future. The late Dr Chris Evans speculated on such an invention in his book *The Mighty Micro*. Imagine an object the size of a cigar box and not dissimilar in appearance to a conventional hardback book. Under the hinged lid or cover would be a keyboard into which could be plugged a silicon chip; facing it, on the inside of the lid, a visual display unit for the presentation of text. Each chip would contain a complete text and it is estimated that the cost of production (though not of sale) would be minimal compared even to the paperback. It has been suggested that the advent of this new development is further off than it need be because of economic factors, and because publishing houses fear the effect on conventional book sales, especially on the paperback market where their profits are largely based.

Bearing in mind present facts and future possibilities, the following pages attempt to consider what the implications might be for the nature of fiction, for its readers and for the teaching of fictional text once it is stored and presented via a microprocessor-driven visual display unit.

Reading and enjoyment

If a reader's response to a text is to be a full one, a major initial requirement must surely be that his or her attitude set is positively oriented towards the pleasure that reading can offer. The electronic medium can be both novel and a novelty. It can present text in a form devoid of the connotations associated with the traditional prose artefact. So readers alienated by conventional books might react differently to a new medium, and even poor readers may respond positively to the presentation of text through a medium in which they have not failed. The connotations pertaining to electronic print are concerned with contemporaneity rather than with the stultifying effect occasioned by the 'great tradition' of literature. They are also concerned with leisure and the pursuit of enjoyment. The same technology brought electronic gaming, so the techniques the medium employs through interaction, and also simply in the presentation of text, can heighten the expectation of fun and ameliorate reading difficulties. It can afford new types of reading experience and deepen response.

Earlier in the chapter I considered how a computer can present text in variable founts, colours, sizes and spacings to allow readers to select a display format suited to their own individual preferences. The facilities are likely to make this print medium attractive to readers, particularly where reading difficulties are normally experienced. The potential is not confined to text alone. The inclusion of textual illustration has always been used to assist meaning and to make a text more attractive. Electronic texts can be interspersed with pictures and diagrams. The development of high resolution graphics now enables those graphics to be animated if so desired. Early reading software, being marketed as interactive story-books, is already beginning to appear. A visual narrative is displayed on screen, stopping occasionally for the reader to participate in some of the protagonist's adventures. A video disk could go further: each video frame could combine text or real-life picture, or a combination of both. It is also possible to intersperse or combine in the same frame live action sequences and pages of static text. All this is capable of enriching readers' experience by making the text more attractive and at the same time more meaningful.

Responses to fiction

The acquisition of meaning could be said to be the major function of the reading process, operating at a number of levels, from the individual word to the text as an organic whole, and from the literal to the evaluative. Teachers use comprehension exercises regularly to ascertain the nature of response among pupils. On a computer, at least the literal and inferential forms of comprehension exercise can easily be programmed. Again, commercial software is already being produced along these lines. Read-along audio tapes of stories are accompanied by computer programs to measure comprehension in the understanding of main ideas, sequence of events and the separation of literal from inferential and evaluative information. If we are considering the presentation of electronic print stored in the same data bank or available in the same medium as the comprehension activity (unlike the audio tapes), there is no reason why interactive tasks cannot be inserted in the text as relevant points. Multiple choice comprehension, cloze procedure, sequencing and prediction could all be included. These activities need not simply test readers; they could help clarify what they have read. According to their response, readers could be sent to appropriate parts of the text – continuing with the narrative if performance is satisfactory, or regressing to a relative passage of text if certain clues have not been picked up.

Reading is not, after all, a linear process on a temporal plane alone. It is rather a psychic process and involves the oscillation of anticipation and retrospection. Prediction and regression are a characteristic that may be observed at all levels of reading. As we have already seen, in decoding symbols the eyes oscillate in their fixations while the mind retains clues towards meaning from the immediate context. Similarly readers may turn forward or backward in the text to clarify or to reinforce already existing contextualisations. Both physically and mentally, able readers can manipulate the linearity of the textual narrative, and they do this despite the predetermined physicality of the text that persuades them to read from left to right, from top to bottom and from front to back through a book. In contrast to this, an electronic text reveals no such necessary disposition. Being totally unlike the conventional form in the way it is stored, it should bring with it no conventional expectations. It can be manipulated to contravene naïve intuitions and to inculcate and foster the strategies that really underlie the reading process.

While these strategies replicate much that is characteristic of the normal response to fiction in the mind of the reader, as specified and defined explicit activities programmed into an electronic text they could well interrupt the response of readers and even alienate them from the text. Perhaps this is less true of 'interactive fiction' where readers are asked to participate in the narrative. When they are asked to undertake more overtly structured activities, alienation is more likely. This is particularly so if readers have to move from one medium to another – reading a conventional book and then undertaking a computer activity or vice versa. Reading is an active rather than a passive process, however, and the interaction of reader and text via computer is capable of highlighting, if not extending, this aspect of the experience. Coupled with the novelty value of the medium and the activities involved, the interactive demands made upon readers might well motivate and involve them with the text more rather than less, even if they do not necessarily reduce readers' psychic distance from it.

Approaches to reader involvement

This involvement can be developed, and it is here that psychic distance may be reduced. If, for example, readers are asked to predict future events, why should the writer not allow these events to occur? The novelist John Fowles among others has already experimented with alternative conclusions to his work, giving readers what amounts to two different endings in *The French Lieutenant's Woman*. Some publishers have experimented with programmed fictional narratives (in hard copy) where the plots develop according to limited reader dictates. The books are in the form of branching texts: at selected points in the tale, readers are given a multiple choice selection of ways the narrative can develop. They then turn to the respective page indicated and continue their chosen version of the story. In principle the idea is attractive but in practice the paper medium has always been a little clumsy for this sort of thing. The computer is more suited because of its text-handling capabilities, interactive facilities and lack of predisposition towards sequential linearity.

To some extent, readers are already able to experience such situations in textual role play and simulation software. A closer experience of narrative can be obtained from an adventure game. This genre of software was first developed for a mainframe computer at Stanford University in the United States by William Crowther and Don Woods. It was later developed by Scott Adams, who has now written a number of classic adventure games for microcomputers. An adventure program first defines a situation, identifies the user as protaganist and specifies a quest. The user then embarks upon this quest from a starting point somewhere in a micro-world held in the computer's memory. The starting location is described on screen in words (and increasingly in pictures) while the computer waits for the user to decide what action to perform. The action (for example, 'go north') is then keyed in, and the computer responds by telling the user in words and/or pictures where he or she is, who he or she meets and anything else that happens as a result of his or her actions. Users can collect and discard items, open interesting doors, examine curious objects and generally perform a range of other activities.

Each program is different not only in the location, theme and task(s) but also in the vocabulary the computer will understand and the actions that may be performed. Part of the strategy is to discover which words the computer has been programmed to accept. Thus the narrative is constructed action by action, episode by episode as the user explores the micro-world the author has constructed. The games are exceedingly complex and can take many hours to play – each adventure with the same program being different because of the varying performances of the user/protagonist each time the game is played. In effect, what is occurring is the evolution of a narrative as defined by the program writer, but it is a narrative in which the reader can really feel involved.

This is analogous to the reading of conventional fiction, where readers find their sympathies closely engaged with a protagonist. Their feelings move in responsive harmony as they are inveigled by the narrative mode into seeing events through the protagonist's eyes. A computer can allow readers to identify even further with characters and to participate actively in the advancing narrative. It is able to supply and intensify the kind of emotional satisfaction or instinctual gratification that readers require of their fiction. There is, according to W. H. Auden, in each individual the desire to make new secondary worlds of our own or, if we cannot make them for ourselves, to share in the secondary worlds of those who can. For children in particular, a major motive leading them to prefer their favourite books is the desire to obtain vicarious imaginative satisfaction of a wish-fulfilment kind. Frank Whitehead even goes so far as to say: 'This sympathetic emotional involvement on the part of the reader represents the continuity between fiction and day-dream and seems to be, for most children, the "bait" necessary to induce them to want to read at all.'[12]

A computer might allow readers to enter more fully into the secondary world of a writer and also to help more actively in its creation. Far from alienating readers, a computer can be capable of reducing psychic distance so that readers seem a very part of the world they are creating. Whether by graphics or by text, or a combination of both, readers' interaction can be such that their existence is expressed in terms of a secondary world.

The need for detachment

Psychic involvement can become so great that it takes on obsessively psychotic characteristics. Such involvement with some electronic media is not unknown, and researchers have often suggested possible links between psychological disorders and the media themselves. Whether such claims can be substantiated or not, the processes involved in educated reading still impose upon all readers a necessity for detachment. They must be able to adopt a spectating rather than a participating role if a mature reading response is to be reached. In reading a novel, readers are normally conscious of distance between themselves and the events. Fiction becomes a convention of communication with each reader an interested onlooker to whom events are related by the author. Writers offer their readers what they claim to be a possible experience (allowing for the willing suspension of disbelief) and convey what they regard as appropriate attitudes towards events, characters and actions. It is for readers to accept or reject a writer's evaluative judgements of the events described. So despite their involvement with the text, it is important for readers to remain aware that it is 'only' a story. Without this, they are not free to contemplate and evaluate what a writer has to offer. Arguably, these evaluative judgements, rather than any gratification or wish fulfilment, affect readers and, so many teachers of literature would argue, should form an important residue in the mind after reading a book.

The interactive electronic narrative

As a convention for enlarging the scope of the discussions we have with each other about what may befall, a book is a one-sided affair in which readers cannot answer back. Interaction between user and computer no longer confines readers to this receiving end of communication. A form of direct response, if not dialogue, is now possible between reader and writer. A branching program of text can cater for the varied responses of readers. If a text is presented in this form, readers can be consciously asked to accept or reject, the latter not leading now to alienation or rejection of the text but rather to a possible programmed revision of the narrative.

Narratives in the form of adventure games and branching stories allow readers to exercise tentative hypotheses they have about the experiences they encounter. It is common for teachers to invite pupils to respond to texts by discussing or writing about the books they read. Children are asked to imagine alternative narratives ('What would have happened if . . .?'); to predict the future course of the narrative; to identify with personae and re-write the story from one particular character's perspective. The electronic medium allows readers to fulfil many of the aims of these activities but to do so keeping in close liaison with the thoughts of the original author.

The medium can also allow pupils to move into more original avenues. It is now possible to buy software that permits users to generate their own branching programs and adventure games. These can be used to incorporate narratives children have read in conventional books. If the children are allowed to build their own micro-worlds and branching stories around books they have read, they will be encouraged to explore the original text and to consider it critically. This type of software is fairly easy to use and needs no programming knowledge. In designing their own programs, users will thus be able to concentrate on literary aspects like character, motivation and plot and to reflect upon and construct alternative representations of experience to those the author has defined.

The reading of narrative fiction ought to set up and maintain a constant interplay between imaginative involvement and impersonal detachment. This fusion of roles makes it possible for narrative in general and for fiction in particular to exert such a far-reaching influence upon readers, providing them with both entertainment and enlightenment. Electronic narratives could provide great and new forms of imaginative involvement while at the same time be so designed that they require readers to stand back and evaluate the situations before them. They could provide a totally new and different kind of reading experience. Whether this experience will still be one of interpretation, whether readers will be making new secondary worlds of their own or sharing in the secondary worlds of others, is still uncertain. What is just as significant for the present purpose, concerned with the teaching of reading, is whether this new medium might blur the distinction between reader and writer and between narrative text and the reader's own personal reactions. Many teachers see the ultimate aim of a reading curriculum as an encounter with literature in which readers are able to recognise that authors present an artefact in their own inimitable written style and containing their own evaluation of experience. If authors no longer help their readers to see this clearly, or if their vehicular medium prevents them from doing so, it remains the responsibility of teachers (as has always been the case) to ensure that readers see fictional narrative for what it is. Whatever else users of a computerised narrative might gain, it is important that they can experience and appreciate the presentation of fictional narrative as a convention – one that, after consideration from a number of vantage-points, can be applauded or rejected by the autonomous reader. To lose either the convention of fiction or the ability to read it as such would be a great loss, no matter what else might be obtained by way of compensation. Fortunately a computer can be programmed to provide its own means both for the enrichment of the literary experiences that readers are already offered though conventional books, and for the extension of these experiences beyond those that have already been imagined.

A new literacy

In this chapter we have begun to explore how electronic technology can be applied to the activities of present reading curricula. We have also considered how reading curricula might have to alter in the future. Teachers need to look at the reading skills demanded of pupils in and out of school, both now and in the future, so that they can begin to predict what to teach. Teachers need also to look at technological advances to see if any developments can help them teach present or future skills more advantageously.

Some pupils will already have access to computers in other parts of the curriculum. Are the literacy skills already taught them sufficient? If they are taught to read conventional print media, will there be a transfer of skills to the new? If they are taught reading skills via a computer, will there be a reverse transfer? Are some reading skills medium-specific? There are many questions and much uncertainty. Perhaps even our theories and definitions of verbal literacy need revision. The overall concept of reading as a process for the acquisition of meaning will no doubt remain true, but in order to apprehend that meaning it is likely that readers will undergo new reading experiences implicating a modified set of reading sub-skills. At the levels of perception and decoding, literacy is now concerned more than ever before not only with symbols on pages; it must now also include the ability to deal knowlegeably with all the communication media capable of carrying print, as well as higher order skills that we formerly associated only with hard paper copy. Information access and retrieval skills are now applicable in wider diversity to the new electronic means of data storage and display. Possibly, literacy now needs to embrace skills that were simply irrelevant or non-existent before the advent of information technology.

Luckily, the technology offers tools for meeting the linguistic demands it makes. Marshall McLuhan prophesied that we would be challenged by a new electronic technology that would threaten 'this ancient technology of literacy'.[13] Instead we are faced by a technology challenging us to extend present levels of literacy. Teachers are faced with a medium that may help them teach literacy, while extending and increasing the importance of literacy for members of our technological society.

3 Computers and writing

The most common form of human input to a microcomputer today is via an alphanumeric keyboard. This has implications for the writing skills being developed whenever pupils interact with a computer, let alone whenever we explicitly ask them to engage in some form of computerised writing activity. We will need to remember this when considering the relation of computers to the acquisition of writing skills. Computer usage may perhaps lead eventually to a reduction in the use of traditional orthographic skills – at least in occupational activities. Whatever happens, many of the sub-skills of writing are relevant no matter which print medium a writer is using. In this chapter we explore how microcomputers can be exploited to develop general writing skills; and we consider the implications upon the writing process, now that we have electronic transcription and composition systems and interaction with keyboard-type computer input.

Writing and the other language modes

For young language learners, writing commences as an adjunct to other language skills. As part of the phonological aspect of reading, children will have come to recognise symbol-to-sound relationships as they decode the characters. Now they must come to perform the reverse, as they hear sounds, repeat them themselves, identify specific graphical representations of them and encode the sounds in symbols. The process is not confined to early writers. When confronted with a new word to write, adults tend to vocalise it (albeit internally) in order to apply generalisations about graphic representations that they have made from previously acquired data. Punctuation, too, may depend on sound as much as on sense or syntax – witness the use of the comma.

Immediately a problem arises. Computerised speech is not yet at the stage of development where it can easily and widely be utilised in present hardware. This is not to say that it is impossible to use other sound sources in conjunction with a computer. It would be possible to

61

use the 'sound through' system of some computers, which pass recorded sound from cassette to the speaker of a television interfaced with the computer. It is also possible to control a tape or video disk from a computer to provide a speech accompaniment. This sound track might be used as a subsidiary enforcement to other work or it might be integral to the task. Users might be asked to key in letters in response to hearing their names or phonic value, or they might be asked to spell individual words and so on. Some portable devices making use of computer-synthesised sound are now appearing dedicated to letter recognition and spelling drill. The quality of speech is still poor, but the machines demonstrate some of the advantages of solid state technology. They have random access to data, so there is unlimited opportunity for repetition and reinforcement of sound. At the time of writing, we are seeing early versions of voice chips for inserting inside computers and peripheral speech synthesis devices for use alongside. Further research is being undertaken into the production of speech from allophones, the constituent parts of speech sounds. Soon it may be possible to utilise speech in software for writing development. This is assumed in some of what follows, though much of the work may be usefully and sometimes advantageously undertaken without any computer speech facility.

Letter formation

The use of a computer for the teaching of writing might well arise out of, and proceed alongside, some of the letter and word familiarisation programs outlined early in the last chapter – especially when the medium permits the incorporation of a phonic element. Following on perhaps a program matching letter to letter, work might begin with the demonstration of symbols on a visual display unit with their oral representation being heard simultaneously. This could be followed by the learner selecting an appropriate graphic symbol from a range of distractors, which is best conducted using a screen with some peripheral device attached. A light-pen, joystick, paddle or mouse will allow the user to select an appropriate symbol on screen. The use of a touch-sensitive pad with an overlay will permit larger and fewer symbols than appear on a conventional keyboard. This device will also permit a range of graphic character alternatives to those on the keyboard, including representations of handwritten symbols. Initial practice might leave the chosen letter on screen to be matched against itself in a sequence of other letters in another part of the screen. With greater proficiency, users should be able to identify a character after the original has been removed from the screen or simply in response to its sound equivalent. Programs might then limit the time for response as a prompt to greater efficiency.

Using the same type of software, a keyboard might then be introduced. The task now is to correlate a key with the visual display of a character or its sound representation. This activity might begin with the utilisation of only a limited number of keys, and even these might be covered with masks depicting variant letter shapes – lower case, for example, or a closer match between screen and key fount.

From a one-to-one correspondence, users can move on to more complex graphic representations of sounds. This will include the use of different sounds for one symbol and multiple symbols for one sound. When this graphic representation is in the form of words, there is no need for the whole word to be input. A word may be shown with letters missing, so users can concentrate on perhaps one particular phonic structure – such as 'tele*ph*one'/'*f*eel', '*ch*oose'/'*c*oal'/'*c*eremony', '*y*oung'/ 'sk*y*'/'mess*y*'. At the same time, however, some of the earlier software strategies might now be presented using whole words for learners to select from a menu, or to key in, themselves.

While such activities are proceeding, there will be a need for practice in letter formation. This will help to reinforce letter shape but also help distinguish between printed and written graphic forms. The ability to perceive that letters and words have the same function and value in different presentational locations is a difficult conceptual skill to acquire. A computer can provide yet another and important location. It can also present letter shapes in a variety of founts including approximations to handwritten characters if its graphics potential is brought into use.

The graphics potential of a computer also means that letter formation can be demonstrated. The advantage of a computer is that the demonstration can be repeated many times – each demonstration being consistent and identical to the last – until a pupil has acquired proficiency. The computer can also provide demonstrations that vary: slow and large to start, becoming quicker and smaller until they replicate the size and speed of fluent writers' work.

Monitoring by machine

The use of a light-pen here might be advantageous so that users can trace the shapes on screen under machine supervision. A light-pen, however, can go little further than reinforcing letter shape and direction of flow. Its lack of sensitivity normally requires that letters are large. Being operated on a vertical screen, it has little to do with the motor activity associated with handwriting itself. A touch-sensitive video screen could also be used but again it suffers from the same constraints. The use of a graph plotter could more nearly demonstrate the conventional use of a pen or pencil, while a touch pad or graphics tablet could monitor letter formation. With a graphics tablet, the signals are propagated in the surface of the tablet and coded in such a way that a receiver above the surface will pick up the signal indicating where it is located. The receiver is usually contained in the tip of a stylus; and, since the lines are typically ruled at 100 to an inch, the device is suitable for monitoring the precise motor activity associated with users' manipulation of a pen- or pencil-like object. The practicality of this method has already been revealed in a trainable character recogniser whereby a graphics tablet could recognise characters sketched by users as commands for action.[1]

This monitoring is important. The teaching of writing, like many other language skills, is basically a question of initial demonstration and subsequent practice. A computer not only facilitates this, but can also give more attention than a teacher can afford to each pupil's particular difficulties. This is especially true of the early stages where the problems tend to be mechanical: an inability to perceive small differences in letter shapes; or an inability to form shapes, space them correctly or keep them in a straight line. A computer can monitor minute malformations and errors such as might be missed by a teacher unable to supervise each and every pupil's writing all the time.

The display of letter formation and subsequent practice could begin with the letters themselves categorised according to their use of lines, curves and a mixture of both. It might begin with the writing of whole words. Later, a computer will be important to monitor practice in likely areas of confusion that might arise from either approach: *n/m/h, d/p/q*, 'that'/'what', 'these'/'those' and so on. After initial demonstration on screen (or graph plotter), users could copy using a light-pen or graphics pad. Alternatively, they might be asked to trace over the letters of a template spread on top of a graphics or touch-sensitive pad.

Users will need to be encouraged to make 'pen' strokes without hesitation. To facilitate this, the rate of letter formation display could increase in pace as the computer monitors and detects users gaining in competence. The opportunity for response could be similarly determined. It could be defined by teacher before any hands-on experience, or it may vary in run according to user performance. If a screen is being used for display, it would be possible to remove a letter, sequence of letters or word while users attempt to reproduce it. Not only might this develop greater speed: it could also assist spelling. It is likely to give practice in memory recall and encourage mental retention of the visual pattern of letters and words as a complement to the phonological spelling skills applied by competent spellers. With words, writers will need longer to perceive the item to be copied and also to write down. During this time the word might therefore be pronounced to refresh their memory as well as to reinforce graphic and phonic correspondence. Alternatively, or in addition, a related picture to reinforce meaning might replace the blank screen while they write.

These techniques might also be applied in the use of a keyboard. The letters or words might have to be removed from the screen by the depression of a predefined key before users can proceed to key in from memory what they saw on the screen. The program might remove the display automatically after a timed exposure. The technique will reinforce not only letter and word shapes but also letter sequence or spelling. The same techniques could be used for whole sentences to encourage good spelling, correct punctuation, awareness of syntax and, possibly, the appreciation of style.

Spelling

A computer is well suited both to the manipulation of characters and to their display, so it lends itself well to many spelling and alphabetical activities. Sequences of letters may be stored in a computer memory as character strings. Since this representation is almost identical to the real data itself, it can be used for any basic linguistic processing including that of user input of characters or longer lexical items. String programs can thus be written to look for particular characters or character combinations in any text already within the computer's internal or external memory store or keyed in by the user. A computer can therefore match a displayed character string against one typed in to check spelling; segregate and fragment strings as in the separation of base words from suffixes or verb stems from case endings to show the internal structure of words; re-order characters for alphabetical sequencing or anagram solving and so on.

Spelling puzzles and games

There are a number of programs on alphabetical ordering that demonstrate, simply, a computer's facility for such tasks. Some present series of random letters that users must place in correct order. The more difficult versions do not provide any on-screen help in the form of a menu of choices from which to select; instead users are left to key in the next letter from memory. More complex programs take a sequence of words selected at random from an inbuilt database or input by the teacher and hide them in a letter grid on screen, filling unused grid locations with random distractor letters. The words may be printed horizontally, vertically or diagonally, which makes the user's task of finding them more difficult.

Some versions of this program offer the option of a printout of the screen display. This extends the activity beyond direct hands-on experience of a computer, and allows the teacher to use the computer simply for the generation of materials for language work – a facility that is all too rare in current software. A computer used in this way can produce a limitless number of different worksheets simply by organising the raw data in different ways. Considering the number of computers available per class of pupils, printout worksheets can relieve pressure on the use of this resource. Pupils can often start or finish their work away from the computer, simply using it for essential elements of the activity like demonstration or marking. It is easy to forget that computers can be used for lesson preparation and reprographics as well as for hands-on learning and teaching experience by pupils.

The re-ordering of strings is ideally suited to anagrams. In a true anagram, the new word must be formed from another recognisable lexical item. The computer has no way of recognising the semantic validity of any random sequence of letters it generates. It can only match patterns. It must therefore be programmed with acceptable anagram variations upon which it will draw or which it will use as data for string matching against any new strings it generates. Some programs now available present a word, asking users to form as many other words out of it as they possibly can. The words the user constructs from the original and types in are all checked against an inbuilt vocabulary of meaningful lexical items and rejected if they have no semantic value.

Where anagrams presented by computer are not true but simply random jumbles of letters, some specific use could be made of the facility. If words with similar spelling patterns are used ('knife'/'know'/ 'knight', for example) users of the program will soon become aware of the pattern (here a silent k) as a major clue towards unravelling the jumbled letters. The same process could be applied to final e or to many other spelling patterns.

The computer, then, can only match one string against others that it has been programmed to accept. In this, however, it is very rigorous; so much so that while the attribute is of help in spelling programs, it can be problematic in other software. Too often, a computer fails to recognise user input because it is poorly spelt. In some badly written programs this might still be enough to cause the program to halt or malfunction.

It is easy to assume that the meticulous string processing attributes of a computer allow only for precise and structured software working to predefined rules and data. This would be a misconception. It depends on how the facility is employed. Users could be allowed to make the machine work for them rather than the reverse. Keying in their own words, a computer program could display all the possible letter combinations on screen or hard copy. The computer cannot identify those that constitute recognisable English words, since the vocabulary that would have to be provided for the computer to check every variation against would be too large for any current microcomputer. Textual strings take up a large amount of memory and cannot be stored in sufficiently large quantities without large back-up external storage facilities. The matching would also be a very tedious process. More important is the educational argument: the onus should be on users employing their skills and working with others and/or a dictionary to select only those strings that are legitimate. These strings could then be stored on tape, disk or as hard copy for use in a game or other language activity of the teacher's or pupil's own devising.

An obvious way in which the manipulatory power of computers over language can be used is for the preparation of crossword puzzle games. Most software examples give teachers the option of using a pre-programmed vocabulary set or one keyed in, to generate the word grid. The candidate words are then inserted in the grid by the computer and the final crossword presented on screen. In many cases, the grid can also be printed out for completion away from the computer. Besides the obvious logistic advantage provided here, a printout solves the problem of screen space that most crossword programs encounter. A video display screen cannot hold the grid and all the clues on screen at once. Instead, users must access individual clues to be displayed one at a time alongside the grid. Personally I find this cumbersome and frustrating since I often want to cross-reference or scan a number of clues and the half-completed crossword at the same time.

Much of the software discussed here involves considerable mechanical drill. This is not necessarily a bad thing, for writing as an encoding process involves a very mechanical set of skills. The computer's contribution is that it can perform or demonstrate the skills in an efficient and accurate manner, and has at its disposal a dynamic display mechanism that – in terms of speed, animation and colour – surpasses the conventional media available to the teacher. It also provides a degree of privacy and interaction that the teacher cannot achieve under normal circumstances.

This interaction can be capitalised upon so that even drill and practice activities become more inviting to the user. One of the most ubiquitous exemplars of the gaming element in spelling drill is 'Hangman'. In one form or another the game appears with regular monotony on software lists. A word is taken at random from a database and displayed on screen with each character replaced by a symbol of some sort. The player then inputs letters, which are revealed in their correct position if they are present in the word. If they are not present, a penalty is awarded against the player. Typically, a wrong input results in another piece being added to the image of a gallows and felon being built up on screen. The aim is to use knowledge of spelling patterns to complete the word before the image is completed and the felon hanged.

Use of graphics and interaction

While some language programs may be based on conventional games, others are more original. Graphic games are common, often based on arcade games formats and employing the loud noise and lively aggressive action that we have come to associate with this form of entertainment. Too often, however, the addition of sound and graphics serves only to provide some form of extrinsic motivation for pupils. Absurdity can arise when pupils deliberately set out to fail because the special effects are so much more spectacular when they do.

More interesting is the software that uses computer graphics and interaction to highlight salient language features, thus making the game integral to the learning process involved. This can be explicit demonstration but it can also be built into game-type software. One graphics program is set on a building site where users have to build compound words. Another uses a bulldozer to join letter combinations together into words. A third is set in a zoo where users are asked to group words in cages according to meaning sets.

Context and meaning

This software provides novelty and can be a technically revealing utilisation of mechanical skills, but there are important reservations. Primarily, this type of software presents language drills without any form of contextualisation. The words themselves are provided in isolation without any reference to their natural function in language use. One form of contextualisation could be provided immediately. There is no reason why software cannot be designed to allow teachers to key in lexicons specific to individual pupils' needs and interests. These vocabulary sets might be based upon particular terms needed by pupils at any one time for a project or essay. They might also be based upon words they commonly find difficult.

Further contextualisation is also required. Without consideration for the semantic value of words or their syntactic context, the spelling and writing of them can become a mindless activity. It might also become ambiguous, confusing or even erroneous. One example will suffice: many English words are homonymns in need of semantic or syntactic contextualisation before they can be spelt correctly. Without seeing a bottle of perfume or a letter being posted, one cannot determine between the graphic representations 'scent'/'sent'. Alternatively, one needs to see the relationship and function of a word within a grammatical construct – 'you are wearing scent'/'I sent you a letter' – to distinguish correct spelling.

There are a number of ways of providing this contextualisation, beyond reference to a dictionary or referents external to the medium. The graphics potential of the computer on its own or interfaced with a video disk can provide a visual context. Pupils can be asked to spell objects and actions that appear on the screen. These objects can be associated so that a complete picture is built up with a specific vocabulary set. Further software could present other scenes. Some of these might be connected because of semantic affinity or to show transformations. One image could show a cat on the mat with users prompted to supply the preposition. A subsequent image might show the cat beside the mat, and so on. Some images might be shown to highlight specific spelling patterns. To highlight such patterns further, certain letters could be already supplied and users asked to concentrate on selecting the remainder, these being the ones specifically isolated for attention. One successful program I have seen used deletes vowels from sentences of text; here the contextualisation is provided solely by the verbal construct, however, and later software might similarly omit the visual referent. The screen could then present single words within semantic clusters. The words 'bore'/'boar' might be displayed at the top of the screen, and users asked to select the word that suits most appropriately the set 'pig'/'hog'/'sow', which appears at the bottom.

Returning to the simple anagram routines mentioned earlier, these could also benefit from verbal contextualisation. Specific words within a presented text could be jumbled and users asked to spell them correctly. Further verbal contextualisation could be offered through the presentation of cloze procedure exercises. Again, a semantic context could be provided as in 'the witch was tied to the (steak/stake)'. Or users could be asked to use syntactic clues to choose between 'I went to (their/there) house'.

Extended texts rather than individual words will tend to make language activities more meaningful to children. This is particularly so if the texts can be related to children's educational needs or to their other activities, in class or beyond. There is no reason why longer texts cannot be input in the same way as proposed above for use with isolated word sets. With my software, it is possible for whole frames of text to be typed and saved electronically. They might be discrete or sequential, original writing by a particular pupil or a transcription from another book (fiction or reference) used in the classroom. Whatever their source, they will be suited to the child's interests and linguistic needs at that time and matched to his or her ability. These texts can then be loaded into a computer and used with any one of a number of language programs since they are all compatible.

One program will select individual words from the text (chosen according to parameters specified at the start of the program) and present these in a 'Hangman'-type activity. Another will jumble the letters in these words. Another will replace the whole text with asterisks and ask pupils to reconstitute the text letter by letter, wherever they can recognise particular words or spelling patterns. In each program, the activity has a meaningful context. Pupils are working on real sustained texts that have an interest and/or suitability for them. At any time, they can recall that text for reference.

Oral contextualisations are also relevant. When the state of the art permits, computers will be able to provide spoken contexts for spelling activity. Again, this should not be confined to spelling tests of individual words. Larger contextualisations could eventually become possible.

Punctuation

Punctuation and grammar are important to the writing process. Both are susceptible to precise rules and therefore amenable to software application. In addition, a computer can handle punctuation and spaces within character strings with the same facility as letters.

Punctuation exercises and games

As a routine exercise for the use of capital letters, lists of nouns can be displayed on screen and users asked to identify those that are proper nouns warranting an upper-case initial letter. While this exercise can be conducted in a number of ways, including with the use of a peripheral device, it is probably best conducted as a string matching exercise in which users are asked to key in the word using upper- and lower-case characters. The multiple keystroke required to produce the upper-case symbol (normally a shift and character key depression) is likely to enforce the use and differentiation of upper and lower case. Subsequent keying in of the remaining lower-case letters will reinforce spelling and word shape. This same process can be applied to sentences. Initially, users might be asked simply to be aware of the initial letters in sentence structures but later practice might involve proper nouns embedded within the constructs.

Similar activities can be used for practice in the use of full stops, commas and other punctuation, users keying in correct versions of incomplete or totally unpunctuated sentences. The use of a light-pen to identify the positions of punctuation might be another way of practising the skill. The layout of a text might be treated in the same way with users identifying appropriate breaks in the text and with the aid of a keyboard or other peripheral device, manipulating the display of direct speech, script, paragraphing, letter headings, subscripts and so on.

Many of these activities can be built into games. The game 'Space Invaders' is well known for its exploitation of computer interaction and makes great use of the machine's graphics and sound potential. There is now a version in which users score points by dropping punctuation marks into their correct positions in sentences. The arcade game 'Pacman' has also been adapted for the microcomputer. A fiendish screen character moves along the text, devouring capital letters and punctuation marks before spewing them forth at the end. Users must manipulate another character to return them to their rightful place. The unique facilities of the computer can be used in more sober ways to practise punctuation skills. One of my programs presents texts in which all the punctuation marks, or all the letters, or both, have been removed. Users must then reconstitute the text using all the reading, spelling, punctuation and typographic clues they can muster. One advantage of this program is that it is content free. I can prepare any electronic text I want pupils to use. It is thus possible to copy or construct texts in which particular punctuation skills can be practised; also, texts can be provided that are well suited to the ability of individual pupils or to their interests. Extremely useful is the fact that texts written by the pupils themselves on a word processor can be loaded into the program. These are then manipulated to remove punctuation so the students can see their own strengths and weaknesses in this area as they struggle to reconstruct the text.

In the same way, my students have also used a version of a sequencing program I developed to help them with their awareness of punctuation. I prepared a number of texts in which complex sentences were split into discrete words, phrases and clauses, which the computer then presented for users to sequence. In so doing, they made considerable use of the punctuation clues left alongside adjacent words in the jumbled sequence. A capital letter at the beginning of an item indicated the start of a sentence (unless it signified a proper noun); a full stop after a word or phrase hinted that this item should be the conclusion of the sentence; dashes and brackets at the beginning and end of two items suggested the order in which these should come in parenthesis; an opening pair of quotation marks provoked the search for another item containing the closing pair. Commas, semi-colons and colons also helped in the eventual sequencing of the sentence. Again, it was possible for students to write and load into the program their own electronic texts before working on them in this way.

Punctuation in processing and composition

As well as employing a computer to process text and present it as some form of exercise, it is possible to employ the computer simply as a tool for user processing of text. Advanced software could emulate a word processor and allow the user a number of facilities for the processing of text. Indeed, there is no reason why many activities cannot be provided on a word processor. Texts can be typed in and jumbled by the teacher for later sequencing either back on the word processor or on worksheets printed out from the machine. The teacher could prepare a text that is incomplete in some way, and students could then use the word processor to complete it, inserting punctuation, altering lower case to upper (and vice versa), experimenting with layout until they are satisfied with a final version. This version can then be printed out for marking or circulation and discussion among peers. If a number of students have prepared their own individual versions of the same text, a comparison of these in class can give rise to much worthwhile discussion.

As word processor design becomes more sophisticated, a number of interactive features are being incorporated to help users in composition. The first feature analysis programs can now be loaded into a computer to analyse texts that have been written on the machine. These programs can provide useful stylistic evaluations of sentence length, readability, word frequency and so on. Writers can then act upon these prompts and redraft the text accordingly. It is realistic to foresee a word processor that continually provides a commentary to writers as they compose their text, so that they can revise it immediately. Many users would find invaluable a machine that draws their attention to the fact that the last time they used a full stop was 300 words ago; that the average length of their sentences was 250 words; that they have used only four commas in the whole work; or that the last full stop was not followed by a capital letter. Such prompts could be provided on screen in a small text window separated from the text. The text itself could be highlighted in colour or marked with a flashing cursor to reveal exactly where the problem lies. Eventually, it will be possible for an audio commentary to accompany the writing task on a computer.

Grammar

A range of software can be developed for grammatical skills. School textbooks contain countless examples of mechanical exercises that may be transferred to a computer. Here they gain from novel presentation, structured development and immediate monitoring and reinforcement, though their value might reasonably be questioned even as textbook activities if not treated sparingly and with extreme care.

Syntactic exercise programs

There are already a number of sentence analysis programs in which users are asked simply to identify parts of speech or structures within a particular utterance displayed on screen. Substitution and transformation exercises are also feasible. In the first, a user is asked to delete incorrect words in a sense group and to enter the correct words. In transformation exercises, users can be asked to give the plural forms of singular nouns, change adjectives into adverbs, alter present tense to past tense and so on. At the simplest level, users can be prompted to select the correct transformations from a range of distractors. More complex would be the keying in of the transformations without assistance other than, perhaps, from the provision of an incomplete answer for those experiencing difficulty. Sequencing programs, too, should help in the awareness and understanding of syntax. The program mentioned in the last section that split down complex sentences into random sequences for reordering has proved useful for syntax as well as for punctuation. It is also possible to provide higher order sequencing of sentences to construct paragraphs. A more flexible approach would be to allow users to construct as many sentences as possible from a given set of phrases or other syntactic word groups.

At a higher level still, guided composition techniques for the formal control of writing might find a use. A series of sense frames can be presented in specific sequence such that the choice of any item from each frame in turn will form a logical, connected passage of prose. To begin with, any choice from the frames could yield a correct passage of writing; pupils could choose any item from each frame in sequence and still be presented at the end with a satisfactory composition. Later, however, the choice in the frames might depend upon structural criteria. The choice of an initial noun form will dictate the choice of subsequent pronouns; having selected one tense, students must then select the appropriate verb form consistently in the choices that follow.

The graphics potential of microcomputers is not confined simply to the presentation, animation and manipulation of text. One early piece of software from the United States used cartoon-style graphics to reinforce grammatical function and word meaning.[2] Several printed nouns were displayed on screen. One of these was selected by the user with a light-pen. A picture of the selected noun then appeared, closely followed by a list of verbs down the side of the screen. On touching a verb with the light-pen, the noun acted out the intended meaning of the verb. A subsequent development prompted users to select words from a menu to create a sentence. When all the words had been selected in correct order, an animated sequence demonstrated the meaning of the sentence.

A number of commercial programs now exemplify a similar approach. One shows a randomly drawn face that is then blanked out after sufficient time has been given to study it. Users must then re-create the face by typing in words to identify and describe its salient features. Each feature can be modified through the use of adjectives (including comparative forms). Finally both faces are displayed together with a list of the differences.

Much of the grammar software so far envisaged has been concerned with relatively routine, mechanical activity. Certainly, this would be true of most of the software commercially available. This is not altogether surprising. Microcomputers can only process the quantifiable, and grammar can easily be seen in this way. This is not meant to be an outright condemnation of it: I have given these software examples because I believe there are appropriate educational opportunities for this type of activity. Part of language learning must develop from some form of initial demonstration even if it is not presented as such. This awareness will be followed by competence only if sufficient opportunity is afforded for practice. Remediation of language difficulties is often effected only in this way; but, at the same time, there has been a marked trend away from drill and rote learning – particularly, though not exclusively, among teachers concerned with early language acquisition. Some of this accords well with modern linguistic research in its attempt to present and investigate language within, rather than divorced from, its use in a linguistic context. It also accords well with the current move away from computer-assisted instruction to computer-assisted learning. In other words, learners are released from tightly structured and mechanical teaching to learn more by their own discovery than by instruction. The question is, therefore, can a computer meet the demands of this new situation?

Learning grammar through discovery

At the University of Birmingham, John Higgins has devised some simple programs dealing with the problems of inflectional English morphology, which provide an interesting reversal of the usual expectation that computers should set users tasks for them to solve. Instead, this software adopts an exploratory approach in which users set tasks for the machine to solve. One program's offer is to place the correct form of the indefinite article before any noun phrase that a user cares to key in. On the basis of simple pattern recognition techniques, the program enables the computer to distinguish between such minimal pairs as 'an un-informed person' and 'a uniformed person'. But there are situations where the program does make an error. Such programs might be inappropriate for individual use but they can be powerful stimulations of group discussion, the focus being either to 'defeat' the program by inventing tasks that the computer cannot solve (and reasoning why) and/or to discover the principles the program is applying to produce its correct and incorrect versions. Another program offers to accept any word – whether real or invented – and to add an *s* to form the third person of a verb or the plural of a noun. Users can have great fun attempting to confuse the machine and by inventing their own words obeying the grammatical rules of English.

The new programming language Prolog (PROgramming in LOGic) indicates another way forward. 'Balloon' is a variation on the parlour game in which one person adopts the role of a hot-air balloon owner. The other players decide what objects they wish to take on a journey and the owner dictates what may be taken and what must be left behind. The object of the game is for the players to establish the criteria by which the owner makes his decisions. One Prolog version gives the computer the role of owner while the users input their choices to be told in reply what they might take. Each user then tries to establish the inclusion/exclusion rules by which the computer is operating. In the published version, the suggested criteria include a semantic option (for example, all objects must be black) and a spelling option (one rule insists that objects must contain only four letters or begin with a certain letter). The program is easy to modify so that a wide range of other criteria might be included: other spelling patterns or specific grammatical functions of words (abstract nouns, proper nouns and so on).

There are two significant advances in this type of software. The first is that Prolog programs, being databases established and interrogated in a high level language not too dissimilar to English in logical structure, are easy to access and amend or enlarge. Thus the interaction of the program is user-friendly to an extent that BASIC is not, and the changing of data to accept new inclusion/exclusion criteria is more easily executed by pupils themselves. Further, in establishing the database or inter-rogating it, pupils are forced to classify and categorise. This has many applications across the curriculum – no less in explicit grammar work involving parsing and the grammatical function of words.

Software can be used in many other ways to help users learn about language. One set of unpublished programs I have seen used encourages learners to devise their own language. Users are given a lexicon of invented words grouped according to grammatical function. In the first program they are nouns, adjectives, verbs and adverbs, which users are then invited to construct into 'sentences'. Each program increases in complexity to include further parts of speech and translations from the new language back into English and vice versa. This new language is artificial: it does not have its own structure and rules but borrows these from English. Yet precisely because it does this it is a useful education aid. Users apply their knowledge of English syntax in a novel situation where the emphasis is on grammatical structure rather than on semantics. It is interesting that while this software is still concerned with a very precise and mechanical activity, it is not prescriptive. It would be easy to monitor the user's language constructs for correctness. Instead, the computer is employed to offer the information in a structured way and to provide a printout facility for easy recording of the sentences constructed. The emphasis is upon what users, working as a group, bring to bear and discuss in relation to language as they compose and translate structures or as they later exchange and evaluate hard copy of their work with their teacher or with each other.

Papert, in a lengthy argument countering the type of drill and practice learning activities mentioned earlier, describes a variant approach and draws attention to the success that might be encountered in teaching grammar through cognitive strategies. He recalls a class in which pupils used computer programs to generate sentences, giving a machine the syntactic structures within which to make random choices from given word lists. The result was a kind of 'concrete poetry':

> Insane retard makes because sweet Snoopy screams
> Sexy wolf love that why the sexy lady hates
> Ugly man loves because ugly dog hates . . .[3]

Papert draws attention to one girl, Jenny, who had been drilled in grammatical categories for many years. She had never understood the differences between parts of speech. One day she suddenly said, 'Now I know why we have nouns and verbs.' As she tried to get a computer to generate utterances, she found herself classifying words into categories. In order to 'teach' her computer to make strings of words that would look like English, she had to 'teach' it to choose words of an appropriate class. What she learned about grammar from this experience with a machine was anything but mechanical and routine. She learnt, according to Papert, the meaning of grammar. She did more than learn definitions for particular grammatical classes. She understood the general concept that words (like things) can be placed in different groups or sets and that doing so would work for her.

The use of grammatical models

Further software involving the generation of language might be developed from work in artificial intelligence and natural language processing. If language utterances are presented not as strings of characters but as lists, the elementary unit becomes the word rather than the character. This precludes the string operations underpinning much of the software so far envisaged but it makes possible the imposition of activities at a higher level of structure. List processing programs are well suited to grammatical analysis and, in reverse, to language synthesis and generation. In the 1950s and 1960s, a considerable amount of research was conducted on phrase structure models of grammar since these were the most common way of representing an infinite number of sentences in a small number of rules. In a phrase structure model, each rule consists of a symbol, an arrow and a string of symbols. This representation means that the string of symbols on the right of the arrow may be substituted for the symbol on the left:

S						
NP				VP	S → NP	VP
N				VP	NP → N	
Jane				VP	N → Jane	
Jane	V		NP	PP	VP → V	NP PP
Jane	V		NP	P NP	PP → P	NP
Jane	V		NP	to NP	P → to	
Jane	gave		NP	to NP	V → gave	
Jane	gave	the	N	to NP	NP → the N	
Jane	gave	the	N	to N	NP → N	
Jane	gave	the	doll	to N	N → doll	
Jane	gave	the	doll	to Alice	N → Alice	

The above example is simplified, but phrase structure grammar does provide an efficient model for the generation of random, syntactically acceptable sentences starting with *S* and making successive substitutions. This would be an improvement on current software, which tends to ask for specific parts of speech. These are then manipulated as crude strings appended one to another in print statements, normally in the form:

noun + verb + object

Alternatively, current software might ask the user for specific parts of speech, which are then inserted in previously unseen print statements, for example:

The <noun> bit the <adjective> boy on his <noun>

Amusing the result may be, and users might begin to appreciate the function of parts of speech.

A more imaginative use could be made of language generation programs using more sophisticated software with a phrase structure grammar. Somewhat in the same way that a child learns language through experimentation, so a computer could be programmed to 'learn' language. Words could be keyed in and the computer would then use the syntactic rules programmed in to generate utterances. If lexical items are syntactically identified as they are keyed in, users might begin to see immediately how these parts of speech function. The computer could use the labelled words to generate utterances according to normal rules for each particular part of speech. On the other hand, it might be intriguing for the input not to be labelled according to grammatical function. The computer would then use words indiscriminately. Consequent ungrammatical generations could be identified by the user so that, by a process of repetition and refinement, the computer would eventually be able to apply the correct grammatical function to each lexical item keyed in. The program could build and store a considerable vocabulary through repeated use. At the same time, the phrase structure itself could be enlarged by the student or teacher, perhaps under program control, to allow for experimentation in more sophisticated language use.

A program like this should help users gain greater understanding of the nature and function of syntax. Sometimes, however, the syntactical constructs generated are likely to be odd and confusing. Since the program would contain only grammatical rules of the word-ordering sort, it is possible that an utterance like 'tomorrow I was woken by a silent bang' could be generated. Syntactically this is acceptable; sematically it is incorrect. To obviate such utterances, a set of phrase structure rules is required for every word to tell how the meaning of a word permits that word to be combined in sentences with other words.

The practicality of phrase structure grammars and the programs making use of them depend upon the existence of broad general word categories such as noun and verb, whose roles may be summarised by rules of the grammar. Since these categories seem to be inadequate for a complete and meaningful generation of natural language structures, the employment of phrase structure grammars is governed by certain limitations. This need not detract from the merits of the software. Users might still gain from an encounter with problematic utterances, especially if the onus is upon them to analyse and accept or reject them. Moreover, there is no reason why at least some of the more common juxtapositions cannot be excluded by the program. One current program on which I am working assigns strings of juxtapositions that the user has rejected as meaningless to a database against which all future print statements will be checked on generation before display.

Future developments in natural language processing are likely to help in overcoming the problem of semantics in artificial language generation, though at the moment there is a severe limitation imposed by shortage of microcomputer memory. This prevents any large-scale adaptation of mainframe language processing programs. One development that might prove useful concerns transformational grammar. This grammar extends phrase structure grammar by saying that the latter is operational at only one level of language. This is the base component that can be used to generate strings of terminal symbols and their structural descriptions; these are now intended to describe the unique meanings that English sentences may have rather than unique acceptable English sentences as they would appear in text. They are called the deep structure representations of sentences and need to be operated upon by a set of rules (called transformations) in the transformational component of the grammar before they can produce surface structures that describe actual sentences. Transformational grammar has still not fully resolved the representation of meaning in these deep structures. Chomsky, its originator, proposed one way in his original descriptions of deep structure, though he failed to develop this fully in later years.[4] Some linguists are exploring it further today and there is some work on semantic rules organised in branching trees of semantic categories.[5] These could eventually form restrictions or modifications to phrase structure rules as, for example, part of the base component of a transformational grammar. The challenge would then be to embody this superficially amenable system into computer software.

Language analysis

In the meantime, there has been far more success in the utilisation of computers for language analysis rather than for generation, and this opens up other possibilities for educational software. Even if transformational grammar did reach an advanced state of computer application, it is essentially generative rather than analytical in nature and therefore difficult to run 'backwards'. Attempts to do so have generally resulted in slow, cumbersome procedures. This is not true of more elementary phrase grammar in which there are efficient procedures for running the grammar in reverse; that is, commencing with a candidate sentence and producing its structural description (or proving that the sentence is ungrammatical). This property of grammar is extremely important for practical applications. In education, it becomes possible for a computer to check the syntax of pupils' own writing, identifying errors for correction. It allows for the parsing of sentences so that users can learn from a computer's analysis of sentences, some of which they might have composed for themselves, perhaps even to 'trick' or 'test' the computer. A program could also prompt users to perform their own syntactic analysis, matching user performance against the computer's own processing of the sentence.

Although the memory required for sophisticated natural language processing software has limited its implementation to mainframe computers, simiplified versions could be made available for the micro-computer. Teachers might even prefer not to be faced by sophisticated programs, which might be unwieldy, intimidating and completely over-whelming for some users. The most elaborate phrase structure grammar of English ever implemented on a computer (at Harvard University in the 1960s) had many thousands of rules and often found many different structural descriptions of relatively simple sentences, each one cor-responding to a variant meaning. A teacher might wish to obviate potential sources of semantic or syntactic confusion, even if at the expense of a more comprehensive grammar. Moreover, any attempt to include a sophisticated processor of natural language is likely to bring unsuspecting users into linguistically unfamiliar fields.

One of the results of computer deployment in the processing of natural language to assist an understanding of the way language works has been an increasing evolution of new and exceedingly complex models of language. Augmented transition networks, developed by Woods at Bolt, Beranek & Newman Inc., is one of the most familiar models in structure and conceptualisation to a classroom teacher. The transition network formalism is a diagrammatic representation of language analysis rules similar to those of the phrase structure but with certain generalisations. At Yale University, Schank has developed a computer version of semantic analysis combining case grammar with an extension of an elaborate verb classification analysis, which he calls 'conceptual dependency theory'. Systemic grammar is yet another innovation designed to improve upon phrase structure grammar. It focusses attention upon meaningful components of a sentence rather than merely structural components. The system of choices made by this type of grammar when it analyses a sentence is concerned primarily with major word groupings such as noun group or prepositional group and only incidentally with the details of, for example, the order of adjectives within each group. It might thus be of less long-term relevance to the work so far considered, although it is one of the bext examples of programs that demand and sustain an ongoing linguistic exchange with users and thus call upon many of their writing skills.

Systemic grammar gained wide notices because it was used as the basis for one of the most powerful automatic language understanding systems developed. The work was undertaken by Winograd at Mas-sachusetts Institute of Technology. Here he programmed a computer to work, albeit in a restricted domain, obeying commands to manipulate a mechanical robot-arm to lift and move objects on a table-top (simulated on a visual display unit). The system could recognise and interpret not only complete formal sentences but also colloquial sentence fragments. It could even recognise and select the most meaningful versions of almost all ambiguous constructions. An important innovation of this system was its use of procedures rather than static data structures to represent knowledge. The lexicon contained separate programs to check on word usage while similar syntactic analysis programs 'knew' about each structural form. This complex network of programs was made possible through a new programming language, PLANNER, developed at the Massachusetts Institute, so that special purpose-built programs could be inserted without programmers concerning themselves with all the possible ways in which these programs could eventually interact.

Other artificial intelligence applications

Winograd's work could be adapted to a variety of software allowing users to practise and explore language. At one level, it could turn the random generation of utterances – such as those described above by Papert – into an intelligent generation. This would enable microcomputers to take a more positive role in language activities, possibly monitoring response or simply demonstrating certain language structures to pupils. On the other hand, intelligent generation of language could also shift the critical faculty back from user to machine and so deny users some of the benefits that Papert, among others, sees computers being able to offer. Rather than this, we need to ensure that the application of work from artificial intelligence to educational software permits more meaningful dialogues between computers and users.

John Higgins's work at Birmingham University comes close to the Winograd model in this respect, asking and answering questions within a restricted domain created by the software. On screen there appears a small set of facts in the shape of a table or group of pictures. Users type in a question, which is answered if it is 'sensible' within the restricted domain. Users can also ask the computer to generate a random question that they can answer themselves or get the machine to answer. Another program makes use of a well-known idea in artificial intelligence: on screen there is a room with one door; a male and female figure can be moved in and out of the room and the door can be opened or closed. The computer is programmed to obey commands or answer questions about the display. By pressing the <ENTER> key repeatedly, it is possible to watch the computer maintain a conversation with itself.

Another program from the same source uses simple artificial intelligence techniques to impose a degree of control on language synthesis, highlighting syntax in the process. The program generates two-sentence texts at increasing levels of difficulty. It uses a context-sensitive slot and filler grammar, scanning each generated text for a logical relationship between the two sentences and presenting a selection of logical connectors to users, who must select the most appropriate for the context. It appears that 'the techniques developed . . . would make it possible to generate many millions of even longer apparently meaningful texts'.[6]

Use of Prolog

Semantics might be approached differently via a new programming language like Prolog. This is a very high level language in which statements are reduced to the theorems or axioms of predicate calculus. It is now available in a microcomputer version and has been piloted in British schools, in which a major objective of the trials was to teach the relationship between natural language syntax and its semantics – where as a first approximation the semantics are expressed in symbolic logic: 'This is thought to be an important object in its own right as a contribution to the more effective use of natural language: to teach the distinction between English sentences which are clear and precise and English sentences which are imprecise and meaningless.'[7]

A simple Prolog statement consists of two items and the relationship between them. The objects and the relationship specified can take any semantic form, for example:

clever	means	intelligent
John	is-father-to	Mary
House	is-a	noun

Part of a typical Prolog program might look like this:

Oliver-Twist	has-author	Charles-Dickens
Oliver-Twist	has-type	novel
Oliver-Twist	has-language	English
Wuthering-Heights	has-author	Emily-Brönte
Wuthering-Heights	has-type	novel
Wuthering-Heights	has-language	English

x has-shelf D if X has-type novel

The program could then be interrogated in this way:

Which ((x) x has-shelf D and x has-author Charles-Dickens)

or

Does (Wuthering-Heights has-author Charles-Dickens)

Use of Prolog forces its user to translate informal English into a logic sub-set that is readily comprehensible to native speakers of English, and can easily be used to represent ordinary real-world problems and information. In learning the new language and in representing information in it, users might come to understand more fully not only external data but also their own language and associated thought processes. Sets of facts, arguments and even narratives can be expressed in Prolog. In expressing meaning in terms of the grammar of Prolog, users are forced to clarify their thoughts, to understand the relationships within individual utterances more clearly and the rules and structures of their own native language more succinctly.

As a language of interaction between user and computer, Prolog thus has a number of ramifications for language work, which are likely to increase in years to come. The next generation of computers is likely to employ Prolog-type languages for the structuring of data within computers, and also as a step towards natural language communication with users. We have not begun to consider the sophisticated level of meaning embodied in written and oral form that will be required for communication with intelligent machines.

Prolog is also a very high programming language in its own right, ideally suited to natural language processing. A Prolog program can parse sentences and, while it might not be very efficient, it is close to a specification of the grammar of the English sentences it recognises. Representing the English sentence as a list of words, the various ways in which this list can be segmented represent the various possible parsings of the sentence. The program that recognises sentences like this is composed of rules and facts organised around the parts of speech found in sentences. Prolog can therefore be used in some of the ways indicated earlier for developing grammatical awareness and understanding.

All writing needs not only to be grammatical but also to embody lucid thought and clear connections from idea to idea, from sentence to sentence and from paragraph to paragraph. The use of Prolog could develop this at local level. It might also encourage the development of more sustained thought processes as users learn to compile and work its programs and to query the databases composed in its logic. At the same time, teachers can turn back to some simpler, more conventional teaching techniques. In looking at larger structures than the sentence, sequencing programs will again be useful for they provide examples of how other writers structure their work. Programs using series of sense frames could also be effectual. Unlike those sense frame programs described earlier, these may now contain connections between options based on semantic rather than structural criteria. A narrative that begins with a tailor, a grocer or a butcher will entail later choices between cutting cloth, delivering eggs and weighing meat. Branching story formats will be useful. In addition, formal control over written material might be presented in the form of serial questions. In keying in the answer to each question, users put together connected passages that could then be displayed in their entirety at the end.

While such software will provide a structured development of logical processes for this essentially linear form of thought and expression, these programs might also be constricting. Computers do not need to be so restrictive in assisting the composition of sustained texts, and it is here that word processing opens exciting possibilities.

Word processing

Word processing takes over much of the mechanical operation involved in the writing process and allows writers to concentrate on the thoughts, the semantics, behind the words. When composing text on paper – whether by use of a typewriter or by pen and ink – writers have to concern themselves simultaneously with choosing, editing, formatting and printing the words. The mechanics of production are apt to interfere with the process of creation. Second thoughts about choice of words or the sequence of sentences are discouraged by the logistics of erasers, liquid paper and legibility. The rearrangement of paragraphs is prohibited by the prospect of copious rewriting. By contrast, in word processing the stages of composition and production are distinct and do not distract from each other. The ultimate certainty of effortless production of final copy emancipates thought from the labour of production. Advanced software can even provide facilities to check spelling and punctuation, leaving writers free to concentrate on what they are saying. Such software can also facilitate the search for expression of thought.

Writing requires more consideration than the other language skills. Much material is rewritten several times before it appears in print. It is hard for authors to write down exactly what they want to say without spending time on it. An electronic thesaurus allows writers to move through their text summoning up a lexicon of synonyms to replace individual words. This extends vocabulary, and might also extend thought by providing new images and concepts to the context via the lexicon displayed. Further, the words, sentences and paragraphs may be manipulated, rearranged in new sequences, embedded in other structures, substituted or simply deleted. Writers can experiment with new styles and diverse ways of saying things. Sometimes they can be faced with new meanings and concepts simply by a fortuitous rearrangement of text.

Edward de Bono suggests that far more use could be made of this last attribute of word processors. According to de Bono, the very name 'word processor' limits a user's vision: 'You'd get a lot more out of our machines if you called them "thought processors" and used them for solving problems.'[8] One strategy he suggests is that users key in every random thought they have about a problem and then freeze this list on screen. The list is then refined in the bottom half of the screen, both halves of the screen being scrolled as necessary. Then the top half of the screen is cleared and the short list expanded. Finally the list is reordered before being printed out or amplified in continuous prose on the word processor.

At all levels, from the juxtaposition of words and ideas to the logical development of paragraphs and cohesion of argument or narrative – even for the line and verse structure of poetic composition – a word processor can facilitate both the formulation of thoughts and their expression while taking the drudgery out of the writing process. Writers from novelists to journalists have commented on its potential: 'It so takes the pain out of writing that – I like to think – it removes one of the barriers between the imagination and the page.'[9]

Classroom applications

In a classroom, word processing can have a liberating effect. Conscious choices of language cannot always be made at the same time as the formalisation and shaping of thoughts. The latter come – or so teachers hope – from a deeper subconscious level. Children need to formalise and write down their thoughts and experiences before preparing them for interpersonal communication. For this reason there is a prevalent desire among teachers of the language arts to separate the writing process from the product. A word processor can encourage this distinction, allowing pupils to draft and redraft their work effortlessly and then to produce a variety of versions in hard copy for circulation and comment. A word processor might be utilised further to give insight into formal editing procedures. It could even be used in a classroom for simulation of business situations and newspaper editing or for the printing of students' own books.

Students' willingness to spend more time on process is likely to arise not only because of the novelty of a word processor, or because of its effortless redrafting potential, but also because of the standard of final product possible. A word processing system can encourage perfectionism in formal presentation. The neatness of a final draft from a printer can be an incentive towards mechanical precision in syntax and spelling to match the professional appearance of copy. It might also encourage a heightened effort in content, aided by the word processor's capabilities in that field, to match the style of presentation.

All pupils might be stimulated to write more and better simply by the novelty of a word processor. For the children with writing problems, the novelty might be more significant: it might indicate to them that this is a medium in which they have not failed; it is also a medium that can assist them to overcome their faults, and aid their confidence in expressing themselves. The keyboard can help develop a rhythm in writing. On a visual display screen, word shapes are always identical and so easier to remember. Some software will help children check spelling and punctuation. (Personally, I prefer to see children use the word processor to search their text for particular spelling patterns that they always confuse, so that they can then correct them themselves.) The final hard copy will not betray their poor handwriting. In presentation, their work will be identical to that of their peers. Only in content might it be dissimilar, and this is not to say necessarily inferior – though even drivel can appear superb. Pupils' low levels of literacy might be confined to handwriting, spelling and punctuation rather than grammar or thought, and it might take a word processor to clear the wheat from the chaff and make teachers or other students realise this fact. As Papert says:

> I have seen a child move from total rejection of writing to an intense involvement (accompanied by rapid improvement of quality) within a few weeks of beginning to write with a computer. Even more dramatic changes are seen when the child has physical handicaps that make writing by hand more than usually difficult or even impossible.[10]

The social demand for new skills

In the future it is likely that an increasing utilisation of computers will continue to emphasise the content rather than superficial stylistic features of writing. Stand-alone word processors or microcomputers running word processing software are rapidly being introduced throughout commerce. As well as offering the facilities already mentioned, these systems are able to relieve users of any need to format their text. The medium can handle the layout of letters and reports or make use of other specialised stylistic conventions to produce hard copy in the required format devoid of much conscious intervention by users. Where word processors cannot accommodate particular conventions, it is possible that the conventions themselves will change to suit the medium. Consider, by way of example, the introduction of blocked tabulation in the formatting of formal letters. This followed the advent of mechanical typewriters and is now accepted even in handwritten copy by examination boards.

Where several work stations are linked in a system, then information keyed in can be sent from one station to another terminal without even the need for hard copy formatting. Networks of national electronic mail services are now in operation. A terminal screen with keyboard attached can offer typical word processing facilities including a spelling check, but such systems are also able to send or receive processed text using simple commands like SEND, SCAN, READ or REPLY. Even in schools an increasing use of computers across the curriculum could reduce the demand for traditional orthographic skills. Instead, computers will demand new writing skills, particularly keyboard skills (though even these might later diminish in importance as speech recognition and other means of computer input become more commonplace).

Teachers will need to ensure that students acquire these skills. Keyboard practice has long been taught in secretarial and business courses. Now word processing concepts and skills are fast becoming a fundamental constituent of such courses. It would be advantageous if all children could develop these communication skills. They could well be learning them long before the teenage years when the few who have opted to pursue commercial courses meet the hardware. Keyboard familiarisation is at present experienced on an *ad hoc* basis immediately a child is confronted by a computer. It ought to be more formally structured. It is already implicit in the letter familiarisation strategies we considered for initial reading and writing software. Specific software aimed at developing keyboard skills is also commercially available. The simplest activity involves typing keys to match those indicated on screen. Further software can demand the keying in of longer texts from screen or from texts dictated by computer-controlled disk, cassette and (eventually) from the computer's own synthesised speech output.

Beyond simple keyboard skills, users need experience with examples of the word processing and electronic mail tools they will later encounter. Some software packages have been designed expressly to introduce pupils to these facilities, sometimes from a very early age.

Choice of hardware and software

The introduction of electronic communications into a classroom will need careful consideration of the hardware and software to be used. Few schools are likely to acquire a dedicated word processing system. They are too expensive and can be fully justified only in situations where they will gain continual use. School administration offices are more likely to acquire dedicated machines, and pupils might then be shown the hardware in a real-life situation.

For classroom use, it is more likely that schools will purchase computers for more general curriculum applications and fit word processing packages into these machines. In this case it should be remembered that microcomputers with no more than 40-column visual displays allow only a few words to the line and are therefore difficult to read. More critically, a 60- or 80-column display permits text to be presented with full line width just as it will eventually be printed. One subsequent, drawback, however, is that 80-column displays are less easy to read, particularly on ordinary television sets used as display monitors. A high quality video display monitor, rather than a television receiver operating on a radio frequency signal, provides the best solution. Teachers need to look carefully at the facilities available on each particular word processing package. If the hardware allows, the program often permits users to compose in a 40-column mode from which they must switch to an 80-column mode to preview final format. This has other advantages of an educational nature that are worth mentioning.

There are important distinctions to be made between word processors. Some permit both the composition of text and its formatting on the same screen at the same time. Others provide one mode for the creation of text (normally 40-column) and another for its formatted presentation (normally 80-column). The provision of formatting and input in the same mode could lead users back to confuse process with product. Some writers are effectively able to attend to both simultaneously, but others are not. A writer must engage in a number of tasks ranging from attention to syntax, spelling, grammar and handwriting to the generation of thoughts, integration of ideas into a coherent framework and the consideration of rhetorical purpose and audience. Some of these tasks are more complex than others, but writers have to perform all the cognitive tasks, the trivial and the complex, constituting the writing process if they are to be effective. Inexperienced writers can become overburdened if they attempt to perform them all simultaneously. Using a word processor to format and compose at the same time does nothing to ease this burdern. In many ways, it is analogous to that situation in which a writer opens an exercise book and puts pen to paper: he or she makes a single 'best' copy of his or her thoughts without any previous planning or drafting.

This limited view of word processing can be easy to gain. Many word processors are in fact devices for the transcription, not the creation, of text. They were designed for office use and the bulk of their commands were provided to assist with formatting text. Word processors were originally designed with commercial rather than education applications in mind. They were first seen as advanced typewriters simply to be used for efficient preparation and duplication of unoriginal texts. The design of most word processors assumed that the text had been created elsewhere and that it was simply being transcribed or merged by an individual (the secretary) rather than the author (the executive). In the occupational world, we are moving away from the assumption that word processors are to be used primarily for transcription. On the one hand, secretaries are assuming more responsibility for original input of text as well as for typing and transposing it. On the other hand, managers are beginning to use the technology themselves as they realise the saving in duplicated labour and as they become aware of the new creative support opportunities afforded them if they compose text direct on a word processor.

Approaches to composition

When word processors are designed for composition rather than for transcription, they begin to implement a number of special features of value to the writer. Here I am thinking particularly, but not exclusively, of pre-writing activities. We might easily neglect these opportunities, since such activities do not feature largely in conventional writing classes, particularly in Britain. Teachers might take into class a sensory stimulus or allow writing to develop out of some other activity or personal experience. But little is provided in the way of shaping and refining at the very early ideational stage before writing commences. Perhaps a major problem here is the fact that each writer needs individual tuition at this point, and this is impractical in most classes. A computer is able to provide that individual tuition, so it is worth stopping to consider how it might be relevant.

A small number of language programs have appeared to assist writers in their incubation period. Mostly, these are random ideas generators presenting on screen a series of situations, characters or themes. Sometimes these are closely associated; sometimes the challenge is for users to form an association between them. Too often, such programs are discrete – remote from the experience and ideas of writers, remote technically from the environment in which writers are to work. Even if writers are stimulated by the program, they have then to return to pen and paper. Even if they remain on the computer to run a word processing package, the original software is no longer available to them for reference or further prompting as they write.

The Americans have moved much further in this respect. They have two distinct advantages. Obviously, they have the technology but they also have a methodology for writing based on a rigorous pedagogy. At college level, there is great attention to writing courses for students of all subjects. Heuristic and invention techniques feature large. In the United States, too, the observer will find considerable investment in technology with large computer laboratories and campus networks. The two have come together and there is now an impressive array of research and development projects in progress.

To begin with pre-writing, there are a number of approaches of interest. Some software sets up an on-screen 'Socratic' dialogue between computer and user and might feature a variety of invention techniques well known to many teachers responsible for writing classes in the United States to reflect upon the writer's choice of topic, consideration of audience, the development of attributes and so on. One typical program contains questions based on the often prescribed tagmemic matrix of Young, Becker and Pike to enlarge upon exploratory and informative writing; another uses questions based on the dramatistic pentad of Burke familiar to many writing classes (e.g. scene, purpose, act, agent and agency) for informative and journalistic writing; while a third takes Aristotle's 28 enthymeme topics as the basis for questions upon reasons, consequences, public and private opinions etc. Some Americans are now preparing for the second generation of computer-assisted invention. It is likely to be developed with a greater understanding of research in rhetoric and cognitive psychology as well as a willingness to experiment with the emerging, bolder assumptions about educational computing's capabilities. It is also likely to acknowledge that invention occurs throughout the writing process and that writers' natural recursive habits will need to be accounted for in future writing programs, bridging the gap between invention and arrangement, arrangement and style and back again.

The fact that the US system is based on computer networks already prompts them to think in terms of large systems and integrated software. As a result, the US concept of a word processor is far wider than that in Britain. The UK is beginning to see the production of programs compatible with its word processors to check on spelling. The USA has gone much further along this road. Spelling checkers are commonplace, and integrated programs are now being produced to analyse (often graphically) students' work for syntactic elements of diction, style and grammar as aids for further drafting. Where problems of incompatibility arise, it is the word processor that is jettisoned and another more compatible word processing program encoded. In effect, a number of educators have 'outgrown' commercial word processing packages. Again, this is not just of relevance to education. The IBM EPISTLE system for commercial users is a complete software package to process text for its stylistic and even (within limits) ideational content. The skills American educators are now able to teach on a computer are the skills students themselves will need and come across on computers in many walks of later life.

While it is still easy to see software as discrete packages to perform specific tasks, many US institutions appear to be moving more towards integrated systems. There has always been a danger that computers would emphasise the mechanistic aspects of a language arts syllabus, turning language development into a series of isolated drill and practice tasks. The Americans are now able to provide language activities meaningfully contextualised. Explicit teaching of linguistic concepts arises directly from students' own language use. Initial pre-writing activity on an individualised tutorial basis on a computer leads straight into the writing of a text on the same system's word processor. During the latter stage, further support software can concurrently analyse students' writing to provide immediate and individualised analysis (sentence length, readability level, frequency of word usage and so on). Students can then call upon other software to provide instant tuition and remediation of specific language points. They then turn back to work on their text or command the computer to work on it with them.

How different this is to the tutorial-styled electronic work-book activities – one per program – offered in the past. There are limits to what can be achieved; most obviously, computers can only compute the quantifiable. But as the many software packages now suggest, computers need no artificial intelligence (and that's coming) to look for patterns – whether of spelling, diction or style.

Storage of text

The extent to which we can begin to implement these possibilities is partly constrained by the state of the art of electronic text storage capacity. When choosing an appropriate word processing system, the size and arrangement of the computer's internal store will have an important bearing on the size and versatility of both the word processing package and the text that can be handled. The best word processing system is one that resides in a chip fitted inside the computer. This gives immediate access without any loading delays. In addition, it normally uses none of the computer's own memory, leaving it entirely free for the user's own text. A cheaper and less satisfactory alternative is to buy a word processing program on a disk. It is even possible to buy cassette-based word processing packages to demonstrate and carry out a limited range of word processing tasks. But if a word processing package requires 15K bytes of memory to offer all the facilities required, not much space is likely to be left for text. Of course, if a cassette or disk is being used to load in a word processing program, that external memory store can then be used to store text.

If a microcomputer can be provided with twin cassettes and a controller, one cassette can be used for reading and the other for saving. This permits large files of data to be processed. but the storage and retrieval of data from cassette is slow. The use of a standard disk operating system is far more satisfactory and allows a computer to tackle the majority of tasks associated with a dedicated system. Access time is fast, all texts can be accessed randomly and the disks can hold a very large amount of information. A typical 5¼ inch disk can hold about 70,000 characters, which is equivalent to about 25 pages of the European standard A4 text. The larger 8 inch disks hold some 80 pages of text on each side. A twin disk drive is preferable since copy from one disk to another is a desirable operation from time to time and it is too slow and cumbersome with only a single disk drive. The major drawback of such an adapted microcomputer is only likely to be that the system offers key operations that are more complex and less user-friendly than those of a dedicated system.

Keyboard and printout

Two final points need to be made about the equipment for word processing. The first concerns the keyboard. A full 'qwerty' keyboard layout is probably desirable. There are a number of other keyboard devices appearing on the market. Some offer far fewer keys, but pressed in certain combinations they still offer the full alphanumeric set. Touch-sensitive pads can also be equipped with overlays demonstrating alternative keyboard designs. The argument that proponents of these devices raise is that they increase input efficiency. The qwerty keyboard never was designed to ease human usage. Rather, the keyboard layout was arranged to stop the jamming of frequently used keys on early mechanical typewriters. The convention has remained, despite the new technology's reliance on other technical means of letter formation. If the aim is simply to use a word processor to help in the composition of texts, and if alternative keyboards do prove more user-friendly and efficient, then their use is justified. For the foreseeable future, however, the qwerty keyboard, although an anachronism, still prevails; many, if not all, students should become efficient in its use.

Whatever keyboard is used, it should be ergonomically designed with the keys well positioned and angled. The keys should be large enough to help eradicate mistypings and with enough downward travel to make them firm to the touch. An audible signal confirming depression is reassuring to the user. The function of each key will be partially dependent upon software, but the hardware ought to offer dedicated keys, logically positioned and operated by single keystrokes to activate common functions such as cursor control (for editing), saving and printing. As a minimum, the keys in use should allow a user to manipulate hardware and software simply and efficiently to handle upper- and lower-case characters, margins (including left and right justification), tabulations, indentations, end-of-line determination and wrap-around (the ability to move partly completed words to the next line), insertion, deletion and transposition.

Finally, most word processing benefits from a printout. The desire to see a professional end result is the motivation for most pupils. If this is acknowledged, then it is important to provide a printer worthy of the students' efforts. There are many types of printer available: daisy wheel, dot matrix, ink jet, laser, thermal; only daisy wheel and dot matrix printers have any wide popularity at the present time. They all produce very varied final copy and at greatly varying cost.

The best type of printer has traditionally been the daisy wheel. In its means of character formation, this printer most nearly approximates the mechanism of conventional typewriters. The keys, one per letter, are still recognisably present though they are clustered around a revolving spindle and look not unlike the petals of a flower. The print, too, looks identical to that produced by a modern typewriter. The disadvantage is that these machines are expensive and slow compared to the other types of printer available.

The dot matrix printer is popular, and increasing in quality of printout all the time. Each character is constructed from a series of dots in a matrix. The size of the matrix varies, and this causes a wide variation in quality. The cheapest dot matrix printers have only a small matrix and so fewer dots with which to form letters. The characters are often indistinctly formed, and in some cases they reside above the base line or below the top line so that ascenders or descenders can be displayed. Text from this type of printer is unfamiliar: children can often be disappointed with the look of the product or, worse, they find it difficult to read. To be fair, dot matrix printers are steadily improving in quality. Modern machines have larger matrices and can thus produce more clearly defined characters. In some cases it is increasingly difficult to determine between dot matrix and daisy wheel print. An important advantage of dot matrix printers is that they are also fast in their printing speed.

It would be wrong to assume that all word processing should result in hard copy. There will be times when the word processor is used simply to replicate some of the hands-on activities that other software provides. The use of a word processor for sequencing and cloze procedure are examples of this. There will also be other times when teachers wish to emphasise writing process rather than product. The presence of a printer can sometimes urge students towards a final draft too quickly. In the days before I had a printer in the classroom, I had to ask students to save their text on disk for me to take home and print out on my equipment there. In the absence of a printer, they were far more prepared to spend time revising their work until such time as I could take their disks home to print out. If teachers cannot afford to put a printer in class, it is practical and sometimes advantageous to make more infrequent, but regular, use of a printer elsewhere in the school or at home.

Computers and written product

Microcomputers have relevance to far more than simply the mechanics of writing. A word processor can free users from orthographic and grammatical impedences, particularly where their mastery of them is incomplete. But it would be wrong to divorce style from content. A word processor, in appropriating some stylistic considerations itself, liberates writers to concentrate more on content. At times, a word processor can have a direct bearing on content, processing words to present felicitous sequences of text or new vocabulary that in themselves offer new thoughts (the whole being worth more than the sum of the parts) and contribute to style.

There is nothing new in the idea of a machine's unintelligent synthesis of language. Ahl's twentieth-century computerised generation of poetry derives from John Peters's eighteenth-century proposal for a machine to write Latin hexameters automatically. Steele parodied these devices in the *Spectator*, as did Swift in *Gulliver's Travels*. But it is possible to exploit the apparent absurdity of the concept and its product. We have already considered how computer generation of language could be used in grammar work. Papert, among others, has reported similar work with poetry and story generators, the onus being upon users to reduce or justify computer creations.

The display of text

The presentation of text, whether it is computer or user devised, is worthy of reflection. Word processors allow such ease and flexibility in the presentation of words in hard copy that they could be used to stimulate pupils to explore shape poetry and other imaginative textual formats. Hard copy, however, is not the only form of presentation. Rather its use is declining due to the greater flexibility and efficiency of electronic means of display and, undoubtedly, due to economic and ecological factors concerned with paper manufacture. If we begin to consider electronic textual display, then presentation can be diverse and original. Text can appear in many founts, sizes and colours; it can be animated around the screen; it can combine with pictures and images using the graphics capabilities of a computer. All this can occur in real time, adding a new dimension to the others. Examples of these textual attributes can already be observed in a range of educational and non-educational software where programmers have given thought to the presentation of prompts and other captions to highlight, reinforce or add interest to their programs.

The British poet Roger McGough has offered a more specific electronic 'poem' in the introductory software package that accompanies the BBC computer. To begin with, readers enter their name and then select one of a set of verses. This interaction is continued later when readers are asked to 'help' in the creation of a poem through a series of branching decisions. As the text is delivered to screen, it appears idiosyncratically. Readers have little control over the pacing and rhythm since they cannot control the rate of textual delivery. At times in the program, there is a loop during which specific lines of verse are constantly updated until readers press the RETURN key to continue. These images are chosen at random from a database supplied by the poet. At the end, where the words and images convey semantically a cyclical movement, the text is animated in linear fashion around the screen in decreasing rectangles from its border inwards. The program contains colloquial asides in the writer's own flippant style. These are written in the first person and make rhetorical use of the user's name as previously keyed in. They endow the machine with a 'persona' and add to the use of timing, animation, interactivity and randomisation to give the writing a sense of immediacy, spontaneity and intimacy.

Poetry in particular, with its formal layout, imaginative use of linear syntactical constructs, predilection for visual imagery, rhythm and reliance on succinct and concise use of words lends, itself well to programmed graphic display. First results from children seem encouraging. I have observed work on kinetic poetry in which the character formations were presented on screen so that they depicted graphically the meaning of the words. 'Wash' appeared in a flowing, fluid style; 'fall' appeared diagonally; 'teeth' flashed on and off with some of the letter ascenders representing incisors. From here, pupils can move on to phrases and short verses, attempting to demonstrate graphically the ideas and images involved.

The kinetic display of text is an imaginative use of a computer and a means of expression capable of considerable originality. It extends our present means of written expression. Admittedly, not all children are programmers but they do not need to be. I have seen programs written by children in which other users can input their own words to be animated in particular patterns and with particular pictorial images. One balloon program depicts a balloon floating up into the sky leaving a trail of the user's own words as it does so. Another prints a series of captions input by the user among the leaves of a tree and then floats these words down to the ground as the autumn leaves die. These programs were written by young children with programming knowledge. Their peers were able to use them to create their own original kinetic verses. It would be possible to write more programs containing basic visual images and textual animations as vehicles for pupils to explore.

A more flexible program I have devised allows students to create their own algorithms of animated text and graphics. No knowledge of any programming language is implied. Instead, composers use a small set of English commands that they type in order to present and move their text. Instructions consist of simple commands like

PRINT DOWN IN RED ON BLUE "the setting sun"

or

SCROLL LEFT LINE 2

In this and other ways the text can be printed and moved around the screen vertically and horizontally. It can also be controlled in real time through the insertion of a WAIT command in the algorithm.

This software has been designed to allow students to explore language in an enjoyable fashion. In some ways, the activity can be seen as simply an extension of shape poetry. Kinetic text takes that written form one stage further. This software allows pupils to explore the structure of language in graphic and concrete form, turning verbal images into visual ones and making verbal meaning generally demonstrable graphically. Sometimes the work is entirely original; at other times, students have used the medium to reinterpret the work of other writers in new and often perceptive ways, sensitive to the style and theme of the writer. George Herbert lends himself well to the medium, and I sometimes wonder what originality William Blake would have shown with a computer.

Often the result can be a new textual form. This software is able to combine text and graphics with the temporal element of pre-literary verse forms. I have been fascinated to see pupils become very aware of rhythm in the way they present text in real time on screen. Some pupils have even broken out into spontaneous vocalisation of the texts they read when those texts are presented in a dynamic way on screen.

The same techniques could also be applied to prose, though the larger quantity of data involved at present taxes computer memory capacity beyond what it can stand. In any case, prose might always prove less manipulative simply because of its greater mass and linearity – both concrete and logical. Perhaps more likely would be the advent of programmed text of the type mentioned in Chapter 2.

The 'making' of writing and programmed text

Many writers see their craft as the stripping away of superfluous matter from an inchoate mass and the giving (or rather the revealing) of form. Writers begin with a vast labyrinth of experience, which they refine down before they arrive at their finished opus. Irving Wallace calls each discrete experience a mental playlet:

> These mental playlets, staged in my head, seemed not to result from the conscious me and I would sit in my chair and watch them with my mind's eye as if I were merely a spectator. Then suddenly realising that I was the recorder of the emotions and dialogues and activities of these people, I would grab up a pencil and try to capture what I had just witnessed inside my head.[11]

What a writer is left with, then, is an independent idea or event. Alan Garner, the children's writer, says: 'An isolated idea presents itself. It can come from anywhere. Later, and there is no saying how long that is, another idea happens involuntarily and a spark flies. The two ideas stand out clearly, and I know that they will be a book.'[12] From this 'data bank' of stored memories, ideas and incidents the final work will grow: 'And then, from these hastily scrawled transcriptions I would write with care, applying as much art as I could to these episodes.'[13]

This is the 'making' phase in which writers draft and redraft their narrative. The microcomputer can be of enormous benefit here; but I am thinking of prose in terms of the conventional artefact – a novel, which, it should be remembered, is itself a late arrival on the literary scene. I am still thinking of a single text being the only point of negotiation between the breadth, depth and diversity of writers' experience and the other experience that readers bring into play as part of their response to the work. It is now possible to envisage an artefact at a different point in the process. One can imagine a programmed text in which the mental workings of a writer, before he or she arrives at the final text, may be encapsulated together with data containing all those independent and isolated incidents – or at least a selection of them – that a writer has stored for future use. In the same way that writers work and rework their material, so could users of a program, the manipulation of the data under program control mirroring writers' own handling of their anecdotes and incidents.

It might appear in comparison with a conventional novel that a programmed text is too indeterminate. This, of course, depends on the program. All software needs workable parameters, and it would be for authors (in conjunction with programmers) to define where those parameters should be drawn and what should exist within them. Even if writers wish deliberately to construct a loose model and allow narratives that they have not considered, it must be remembered that the text is not necessarily predetermined by writers' efforts. John Fowles is not alone in refuting such claims. In *Daniel Martin* he makes it clear that while a writer's intention is 'as rigid and preconcived as a piece of machinery or an architect-designed building', there is also a vital role in the development of narrative played by 'accidentality . . . unplanned development of character, unintended incidents and so on'.[14]

Fowles's reference to machinery is apt. Here, he has presented a preconceived model, the programmed machine, but within it the data that can be manipulated to allow for fortunate coincidences and happy pairings of accident.

Writers often begin not knowing exactly their destination. They may have simply an overall conception and a series of images or episodes:

> Finding yourself there, at the beginning of the story, I wanted to start writing at once. I knew there were gaps in the story ahead, particularly towards the end. There was some mistiness elsewhere, as well . . . I don't believe in putting off writing if one really wants to, even if everything isn't fully planned.[15]

So writers begin to 'make' the work their readers will eventually experience. With microtechnology, it is here that readers can join them as writers try to give what Garner calls 'colour to the invisible object so that other people can see it'. It appears that the art of fiction does not begin until a novelist thinks of his story as a matter to be shown, to be exhibited, that it will tell itself. This distinguishes writers from readers: writers recognise that the artistic shape already exists and they seek to give it form; the readers' task is to apprehend that form and assign to it a meaning.

A programmed text could allow readers to experience writers' own searches, commencing with writers' own anecdotes and revelations, and moving towards a realisation of the consummate artefact. The program will allow readers, like their writers before them, to revise many drafts. If the program is well designed, all such drafts will be of merit in their own right. All will approximate to the writers' own formal and thematic concerns; some will even replicate by chance or design the writers' own drafts of their work. But one, and probably only one, will fulfil each writer's obligations to his or her conscious thoughts and creativity. The extent to which readers might be guided towards this singular text is the prerogative of each writer and will depend upon his or her artistic or other purposes. It may be that readers, like their writers, suddenly see a moment of illumination out of which the story must flow: 'I seemed to hear a click in my mind, like the sound of a key turning in a lock, opening something. At last, I saw the way through, that my story could go, naturally, without any forcing.'[16]

Participation of the reader

Such moments of illumination are not confined to writers. Normal readers, too, are susceptible to such flashes of insight. A sophisticated modern reader is perhaps even more so. Far from being confused, intimidated or simply alienated by texts, contemporary readers are familiar with the demands that may be placed upon them; no text is fully determined: 'Everybody knows that competent readers read the same text differently, which is proof that the text is not fully determined.'[17]

The indeterminacy of a programmed text is thus not quite so unfamiliar. Authors have for some time been asking readers to use their freedom in interpretation – even if it means exceeding any limit to what writers were conscious existed in their work. More than this, modern writers do not necessarily aim to determine their text. Writers keep the form open so that readers can become able to participate in the creation of meaning. Readers are granted a greater measure of freedom as texts increase their indeterminacy. Readers of contemporary fiction are urged to be freely creative in the spaces between what the authors determine. Each reader is invited to fill these indeterminacy gaps; indeed, a reader may today be well practised in doing so and may even bring an expectation of such realisation to the text.

As time goes on, authors' need for freedom in their readers appears to grow more insistent. Eventually, readers may be brought to a situation where they are forced to make their own sense of individual works or lapse into incomprehension. Umberto Eco offers a strong version of this proposition:

> Every work of art even though it is produced by following an explicit or implicit poetic of necessity is effectively open to a virtually unlimited range of possible readings, each of which causes the work to acquire new vitality in terms of one particular taste or perspective or personal performance.[18]

Microelectronic technology could simply extend the nature and degree of this performance. It might blur the distinction between reader and writer by forcing the user to adopt even more of this dual role. It might also encourage users' appreciation and understanding of the writer's craft and creation besides offering a stimulating experience in its own right.

Computers as writing stimulus

So far we have tended to consider computers as a writing medium rather than as a stimulus for writing away from the machine. We have also tended to consider them in isolation rather than as part of a wider educational or classroom context. The mechanical skills and cognitive processes that a program may develop and rehearse may find employment elsewhere in written activities, and is important that they do so. The use of a tutorial program to rehearse specific language skills (assuming they are not medium-specific) can be fully validated only if students then practise these skills in their own language use away from the computer. Often the best way of using some skills software results from the teacher's desire to help individual students who have already shown specific language deficiencies in performance away from the machine. After access to a computer for demonstration and practice in these skills, it is important that students are able to leave the machine and exercise their skills in other situations. Activities here can often provide more meaningful and sustained language contexts than those available on a computer.

A computer itself can provoke further writing opportunities to be undertaken once the machine is switched off. Teachers have long used pupils' written work as a means of encapsulating and extending experience. The task has been to stimulate that experience or recall it. A computer may now rank alongside a radio broadcast, television programme, dramatic improvisation, text or class discussion as a writing stimulus. Indeed, it combines many of the effective attributes of each of them in terms of motivation, interaction, involvement and display.

Motivation and imaginative involvement

The very presence of a computer brings a high degree of pupil anticipation and motivation with it. This can be built upon using suitable software. At a simple level, a computer may be used as a presentational medium for text or graphics. This is particularly so when the computer is interfaced to a video disk player capable of storing large quantities of text and still or animated pictures. This alone might create sufficient stimulus for writing. It might also develop the spectators' sense of narrative and give them a structured framework for writing. For inexperienced writers, a more interactive program presenting a random series of images for logical sequencing might enhance their narrative awareness. Moreover, any program that exploits a computer's interactive potential is likely to increase user involvement and subsequently heighten pupil response, to be reflected in pupils' writing.

Games and simulations are useful, since they call for considerable involvement, some of it of a very imaginative kind. Some games require a form of written activity during play. For older students, adventure games might be appropriate. With these, it is always advisable for users to draw maps and keep notes. In this type of software there is also considerable user involvement. Students must determine the course of the narrative and command the computer, acting as their 'puppet', to set out on a quest through a micro-world that is unfolded in text on the screen as they begin to move through it.

The typical form of two-word command language accepted by the computer ('go north', 'sit down', 'examine chest') can provide some contortions of conventional grammar, which might be considered a severe limitation. In practice, it can bring users to a clearer understanding of the function of parts of speech. In addition, the inevitably restricted vocabulary recognised by the computer urges users to extend their own word usage by searching for synonyms and equivalent semantic expressions to substitute for those the computer states it does not understand. More to the point in the present context, adventure games create a strong sense of imaginative involvement. The creation of a narrative with interesting characters and vivid situations in which users are asked to participate can all result in a sense of commitment, empathy and awareness of detail that is fully revealed when players are later asked to write about their experiences. Adventures can be asked to describe in prose or verse a particular situation or character; they can relate their own adventures; and they can redraft their notes of events as diary extracts, write letters to characters involved and so on.

Programs in Prolog might be useful. It is possible to build up a database of characters and events that students can then interrogate to find, say, a hidden murderer. Programs like this lead pupils to speculate as well as to deduce logically. They provide reinforcement in narrative terms of the concepts of causality, motivation and relationship, which can then be used in writing. Some users go on to create their own new databases in Prolog. These are, in effect, simply the basic skeletons of future narratives which pupils may use and which may, or may not, also be fleshed out in conventional prose.

Other approaches to computer stimulus

So much software can give rise to so many forms of writing – notes, secret letters, plans, diaries, reports, stories, argumentative essays and so on. This writing need not be confined to the fictional but can also encompass the transactional, especially where computers are used for information retrieval. Many forms of software demand or give rise to writing situations – both transactional and imaginative – that teachers can use in class. There is an increasing number of published programs accompanied by teacher manuals and pupil worksheets, detailing writing activities to be undertaken before, during and after computer access. Some of these resource packs involve the computer far less centrally than, say, a simulation. Instead, the computer is used more as a tool for classroom management of the writing activity.

Where no such support is given, it is still frequently possible for the teacher to engineer writing situations around computer use. Indeed, this is one practical solution to the problem of computer deployment in class when resource provision is low. Whole class simulations of a newspaper office can benefit from the use of a word processor by a minority of pupils to prepare the 'typeset' newspaper. Class research projects can be collated on computer. A single computer can be stationed in the library, resource centre or classroom on which pupils can enter data from the notes they have made in their researches. This data can be stored in a software database. Alternatively, pupils could begin to build up a project book on a word processor. As each individual student or group brings research findings to the computer, it can be added to the contents already typed in by other students. Initially, pupils tend simply to append information to that already inserted. As they become more confident of the word processor, they tend to insert, transpose and amend previously acquired data so that the computer text becomes a truly collaborative writing activity. Finally, the text can be formatted and printed out as a 'class book' encapsulating a true synthesis of their efforts.

Microcomputers, then, can be programmed to stimulate yet more writing situations in class. Some of these will be new, some will be traditional, but many of the skills involved will be pertinent whatever the writing situation. Moreover, as we have seen, microcomputers can be used not only to stimulate writing activity but to facilitate it and to assist in the teaching of those skills that all writing requires.

4 Computers and oracy

It might seem odd that the skills of speaking and listening have not been considered before those of reading and writing. Speech is, after all, the primary means of linguistic communication and normally precedes the development of literacy. In many respects, oracy is a prerequisite for the efficient and successful mastery of literacy. So there have been a number of occasions when reference to oracy has already become necessary in our consideration of reading and writing with the aid of a computer. The reason for leaving oracy until now is simply that there is far less that can be said of it in connection with electronic technology. We communicate with computers through reading and writing because it is still not possible to communicate so effectively with computers in speech. Therefore, their potential usefulness in developing talking and listening skills is still limited.

Speech recognition

The lack of development in computer synthesis and recognition of speech cannot be attributed to a lack of interest on the part of computer scientists. From the start, they have considered its implementation to be important because speech is the prime form of human communication. Designers have striven to achieve it to obviate the inconvenience of keyboard skills, dependent as they are on the arbitrary conventions of literacy. They have also sought to reduce the degree of user-unfriendliness created, in relative degrees, by all other input devices.

Speech is a sound, a physical phenomenon consisting of waves travelling through the air. The ear detects these waves, translating them into nerve impulses and passes them along to the brain to measure and interpret. Similarly, a microphone also detects such waves, translates them into electrical signals and passes them along to whichever devices are provided for measurement and interpretation. Usually the devices do not interpret the output from a microphone; they merely record it on tape or disk, amplify it for retransmission to an assembly or translate it into yet another form such as radio waves. Virtually all the information present in the original speech is also present in the electrical output from a high quality microphone. The speech recognition problem, therefore, is to design a mechanism that can correctly measure and interpret that electrical output.

It has already proved possible to provide equipment for the electronic recognition of limited speech, and there are a number of devices in day-to-day use capable of being 'trained' to recognise a restricted vocabulary from a single individual with almost complete accuracy. Such performance might be of use in education where a user could be prompted to utter specific sound patterns – individual sounds, words or longer utterances – for recognition by a computer. The problems, however, are twofold. Firstly, the recognition is limited to the speech patterns of a single individual. Secondly, the range of sounds that can be recognised is very limited. For over 20 years researchers have used both analogue and digital computer technology with circuits to detect vowel and consonant sounds, pitch levels, volume, overtones, time durations and a great many other technical attributes of human speech. Yet the most these systems were ever able to recognise was a vocabulary of about 100 different words. The computer could recognise these only if the words were carefully pronounced, one at a time, by one user to whose particular voice the system had been tuned.

Even so, the technology might have application – if not, yet, in a general school context. Restricted sound recognition might still benefit phonic work: initial vocalic generation or subsequent speech remediation. The limited vocabulary size will be less problematic for an early talker whose vocabulary will be small. In speech therapy, a restricted vocabulary of words containing certain pronunciation patterns might be useful. In both cases, the work is likely to be so specific and individualised that the tuning of the device to one unique user will not prove such a handicap.

Typically, the individuals and activities just mentioned are associated with children at pre-school level or individuals outside mainstream education. When it is remembered that every voice in a class of pupils is unique, or that there are some 10,000 English words in common use, one begins to gain a more realistic perspective on the subject. Moreover, listening skills are not concerned solely with sound apprehension but also with its comprehension. Here we are back among the semantic difficulties already encountered in our discussion of writing and natural language processing. In 1970 a committee of computer and acoustic scientists launched a programme aimed at integrating acoustics techniques with the latest linguistic techniques such as those developed by Winograd (see Chapter 3). The aim was to develop a speech under-standing system that closely coupled syntactic, semantic and acoustic components, albeit in a restricted domain. By 1975, a number of systems had been devised. One system, developed in Massachusetts, was based upon the augmented transition network approach to natural language processing as described in the last chapter; but it was highly modified to fit the requirements of speech input. Another, the joint effort of two Californian laboratories, was based initially upon a version of Winograd's language analysis system (also outlined in the last chapter). Again it was modified. It operated in a prediction and verification manner, a characteristic that is significant for our present purposes.

These speech recognition systems do not process language in the same way as described above. Spoken language is a string of sounds, but the processing of such strings from beginning to end in a smooth linear fashion is not practical for speech recognition. Instead, a speech recognition system has to accept a whole statement and then 'think' about it. Which part of the utterance was clearest? Which part was well understood? What kind of words are likely to come before and after that particular word? Does that phrase make sense in terms of the current context? Such systems do not first make a list of all the possible words and phrases that an input sound resembles. Instead, they first use their knowledge of the context of the current conversation – remember, it is a restricted domain – to predict which words are likely to occur and then to look at the sound data to verify these predictions.

The use of a system like this in education will be limited. Any dialogue that the system is able to sustain with a user will operate within a restricted domain. More significantly, even if computer scientists can eventually widen the domains within which systems operate, so that we can provide greater person/machine dialogues, the desirability of too much dialogue might be dubious. It omits the paralinguistic attributes of human interaction, together with the other socialising skills that teachers will wish to foster among their talkers. The essence of human conversation with a machine will be nothing like talking to another human being, as the following simple anecdote indicates. At Carnegie-Mellon University, a computerised speech recognition system was set up to operate within the restricted domain of a game of chess. Sometimes, the computer found difficulty in distinguishing the moves spoken into it and so resorted to its prediction and verification routines to arrive at a particular word. When a user said 'Pawn to queen four', the computer recorded the move as 'Pawn to king four'. The computer could not distinguish between 'king' and 'queen' and assumed that the user must have said 'king' because this was the better move! It will be a long time, if ever, before computers behave in the same way as humans even if they begin to talk, listen and sound like them.

In the meantime, the ability of computers to recognise a human voice in any sustained way is still limited and prone to error. Of more promise, at least in the short term, is the use of speech recognition for work involving a narrow range of specific sounds and small vocabularies. We consider this later in this chapter. Remember, however, that there are now language recognition systems demonstrating an ability to integrate syntactic, semantic and acoustic subsystems with vocabularies running into hundreds of words. These vocabularies appear to be extendible to handle a 1,000 word vocabulary without encountering major new technical difficulties. The outlook for automatic speech recognition in the future is thus far from unpromising.

Speech synthesis

Speech can be recorded and stored in analogue form on magnetic tape for later playback to computer users. The sound might be recorded with a second sound track containing addressing and timing information. The computer then makes use of this information when playing back the tape on a cassette recorder under computer control. Some computers use a 'sound through' system whereby the analogue recording of human speech is stored alongside a program on the same tape. The speech is played back through a conventional domestic television receiver, the sound output to the television loudspeaker being controlled directly by the computer. In this way, only the speech is relayed from the tape and not the program information itself. Such a system has been used in a number of early reading and foreign language programs.

The serious disadvantage of any use of magnetic tape for the storage and production of speech is that it provides only slow serial access to that speech. Access could be considerably improved both in real time and in ease of manipulation through the use of a random access disk on which sound is stored in digital form. The video disk offers fast, accurate random access to any part of the disk. Its two sound tracks can provide high quality stereo sound or dual sound accompaniment to software. Random access audio disks have also been developed. An early version of the audio disk was successfully implemented in the PLATO computer-based system used in Minnesota. This gave access to 20 minutes of high quality speech. Modern audio and video random access digital disks offer up to an hour's recording time. The drawback is that these disks require sophisticated machines to retrieve and playback the sound recording. Even allowing for this drawback, the problems are not fully resolved.

Random access increases a system's flexibility in a dramatic way but the speech is still prerecorded and utterances still fully predetermined. If a computer could be programmed to generate its own speech, it would be able to approximate the greater diversity and infinite variation of human utterances that are possible from the finite number of phonemes which make up the sound patterns of the English language.

Dictionary chips

There are basically two approaches to the challenge of synthesised human speech from a computer. The first involves a specific vocabulary held inside a computer and is thus limited in size by the memory available. Typically 100 words (and their phonetic equivalents) can be stored in a table occupying 2K of computer memory. An additional amount of memory is required to retrieve and transmit the phonetic equivalents to a voice synthesiser. Further memory space will of course be taken up by the program that the voice output is to accompany. It is therefore advantageous if the speech lexicon can be provided in the form of an extra chip plugged into the computer so that the vocabulary does not take up valuable memory space.

The range of words that may be generated using a dictionary chip is limited to the word list it contains. Ingenious users can sometimes form other words, like using the phonic equivalent of the number '2', if present, to stand for the word 'too', or using the letter sound 'U' for 'you' and so on. The fact remains, nevertheless, that dictionary chips are severely limited. As the cost of production comes down, it is likely that users will be able to buy a number of chips all with specific lexicons for different uses. It will also be possible to create your own dictionary chips; but, for immediate ease of use and for general adaptability, speech synthesis reliant on dictionary chips leaves much to be desired.

Allophones

Considerable interest is now being shown in the development of speech from allophones, the discrete set of sounds that comprise speech. This is the second method of voice production. In this case use is made of phonemes accessed via a restricted set of commands. The advantage is that because all speech is constituted from this small set of sounds, only a small amount of memory is required to store the sounds from which a limitless vocabulary is possible. The disadvantage is that the words still have to be constructed. In a dictionary chip the words are already formed and easily accessed. Their individual sounds in combination have been perfected so that the overall quality of speech is high. Stringing together sequences of phonemes is more laborious and the end result does not always sound as expected.

If the quality of individual sounds is still not fully acceptable to critical ears, remember that it is unlikely that speech synthesis will be implemented in isolation. Normally, its educational use will be accompanied by some other form of computer input and output. Hearers are more likely to understand computerised speech if it is contextualised and accompanied by other signifiers of meaning. Also, we are at only an early stage of its development: as quality improves, so speech synthesis will become more useful, and teachers must turn to consider ways in which they might apply it. Even today, speech synthesis will be important if it can enhance current learning activities or if it allows teachers to create new opportunities for learning.

Simple structures of speech: phonemes and words

Spoken language is a string of sounds. Learners need to be able to recognise these individual sounds or phonemes and to differentiate one from another. In normal language acquisition, this is done in a meaningful way so that spoken sequences of sounds – that is, words – are associated with their referents in the real world. In the same way, computers can make speech acquisition and practice meaningful by producing pictures on screen while giving auditory information.

High resolution graphics have greatly enhanced the ability to use pictures on a visual display screen; so, too, has video disk and in this case there is the advantage of a recorded sound track. The exactitute of visual representation does not necessitate such realistic production. It need be sufficient only for recognition and the establishment of a direct relationship between sound and object. The limitation is therefore confined rather to those examples that lend themselves to pictorial representation, and not to the representation itself.

It follows that learners' recognition of sounds can be monitored without requiring them to say the sounds themselves. A program can present learners with a picture–sound relationship, and users can be asked to indicate on a repeat presentation if the correspondence is still accurate or if other sounds have been substituted in the sound channel. Initially, the sound representations will be distinct so that it is easy to distinguish between them. Later software can then present less easily distinguished phonological patterns: 'plane'/'train', 'sheep'/'ship', 'sheep' /'sheet' – always assuming the hardware is capable of making these distinctions clearly audible. In these three examples, the differences occur in initial, medial and final positions. Learners will need practice in all three.

The same technique can also apply in reverse with the supply of multiple visual images instead of spoken words. This would assist in the acquisition of meaning. After correct correspondence of word and image, individual spoken words could be accompanied by the visual presentation of a number of objects, and users could be asked to select the one corresponding to the sounds they hear. Further practice might involve an audial definition of an object rather than the name itself.

Teaching word meanings as opposed to their phonological structure might be further developed not only by establishing the relationships between words and their referents but also by establishing those semantic relationships that exist between words themselves. Words can be grouped together in some convenient way. Then the conceptual difficulty of the meaning relationships existing between the words in any one group can be graded to become progressively more difficult for learners to exercise upon. If teaching is by means of inclusion groups, for example, then 'apple'/'orange'/'lemon'/'plum'/'chair' might be depicted visually and audially, with users prompted to identify the odd one out. Successive stages could substitute the item 'chair' for 'potato' and 'strawberry' consecutively so that users have to redefine more and more closely the meaning relationship that holds the group.

In much of this work, we are dealing with a very early stage of language acquisition, much of which will be encountered in pre-school years. It is appropriate to ask, therefore, how relevant these activities might be at home, let alone in a classroom. With the continued expansion of the domestic market for hardware and software, it becomes more likely that the opportunity for using microcomputers in very early language acquisition will exist there. It is arguable whether a computer ever could, or should, replace language development arising from direct interpersonal contact between children and parents or other family members. It ought to be that computers become an additional resource rather than a substitution for that language learning situation. But it is also possible that the motivating power of computers will prove a stronger attraction for some children, and that parents will encourage this engrossment with machines as a blessed family relief!

A better context for the computer would be where early language encounters with humans are already lacking or deficient in some way or where remediation is necessary. The software described above will therefore have a place in school even for older children if it can be used to extend impoverished vocabulary. Computers can provide the privacy and security that some children might need for some (limited) language development. Computers can also introduce children to objects and concepts removed from their own first-hand experience and which, in some cases, could not be introduced into a classroom in any other way. Computers could come to rival television in the power to enrich and extend classroom experiences.

Because of the developmental stage of the children we are dealing with here, we need to think of some simple means of computer interaction. Eventually, speech recognition by a computer will help solve this. In the meantime a restricted number of clearly defined keys on the keyboard could be used. In some schools I have seen very young children interacting with computers just through the use of the RETURN key and SPACE BAR. These were both clearly marked on the keyboard. Perhaps a keyboard is best avoided altogether and use made of some other peripheral device like a joystick, paddle or light-pen. It is unfortunate that we are unable to make significant use of speech input, which would certainly facilitate user interaction. Its exercise would also facilitate learners' ability to recognise sounds, since the production of sounds is closely linked to their recognition. Recognition is usually a precursor of production, and production a reinforcer of recognition.

As soon as suitable speech recognition is developed, use can be made of this recognition/reproduction relationship. The picture/sound software already outlined could be extended. Users could then be asked to repeat a name after the initial auditory presentation by a computer. If input is unsatisfactory, the routine could be repeated until users are correct in their performance. Here computers offer distinct potential. Each sound presentation can be identical to the last – unlike that from the human model. Similarly, pupil performance would have to be identical each time if a computer is to recognise the input. This could develop and reinforce a speaker's vocal precision. The program could repeat the routine for a number of objects/words and then show the object only, prompting the user to name it. An elaboration of the exercise might be for the computer to present two (later more) possible names, asking users to repeat the correct one. These names would be very distinct. Later, they might have only small phonetic differences to encourage users to apprehend and articulate small sound variations. The degree of proximity between words would depend on the machine's ability to distinguish between them. We are talking, therefore, of software and hardware still some time in the future.

Before there is acceptable speech input, we are more likely to see greater refinements in speech output. The introduction of speech synthesis using phonemes rather than word dictionaries will enlarge early speech work, enabling words to be split up into their respective phonemes for more explicit pronunciation. This will be useful in software that attempts to provide a transition or remediation program for pupils unable to distinguish between words of increasing phonological similarity. Looking at spoken words as phoneme strings rather than as words, a computer will be able to perform its string handling operations to match user input against stored string, phoneme for phoneme. The computer will be able to isolate the particular phoneme causing difficulty. It could then repeat the word, isolating the phoneme with pauses between it and the rest of the word. It could also branch to other routines to give further experience of that phoneme, presenting it embedded in other words in initial, medial and final positions.

In the software so far offered, emphasis has been placed upon the use of pictures as referents and so upon the recognition by users of heard sounds on a sound track where the speaker is necessarily unseen. This has its uses, since it emphasises the relationship between sound and object. Inevitably, it reduces the relationship between the sounds and their originator. There is much to learn from seeing a speaker at close quarters. Children learn how to generate sounds and how to differentiate between sounds more clearly. They also learn how speech is accompanied by gesture, facial expression and all its other paralinguistic features. Computers have little to offer in this respect, but there are also times when a speaker is expressly not seen. Much spoken material comes to listeners via radio, audio tape, television commentary, records, telephones and, in due course, from computers themselves. Here the speaker is not present. Children need practice in listening to sounds from unseen speakers. The important point is that this practice is limited in the early stages of language acquisition. Here face-to-face communication will be preferable.

Variety of language should come not just from its presentation. The phonetic values of sounds are not absolute but relative. Language is based on many different sets of sounds each with its own relative contrasts, so it is important that children experience a range of spoken forms and idiolects. Again, care must be taken to avoid unnecessary confusion and difficulty for early language users. Native Britons are already exposed to North American pronunciation patterns in some of the early electronic devices employing speech synthesis. Perhaps they are not perplexed by the disparity between English and American pronunciation patterns. Perhaps it might actually widen their ability to recognise diverse accents. What will happen when these devices also incorporate speech recognition? Will users be encouraged or required to adopt particular speech patterns in order to communicate with the machines? The advent of printing disseminated one particular dialect and created a standard English writing system from it. It is possible that electronic speech synthesis and recognition could do the same for oracy.

Larger structures of speech: words in combination

If we turn to consider computer synthesis and recognition of larger structures of speech, these facilities may be applied widely to much of the software already outlined in this book. In some cases speech synthesis and recognition will serve merely to enhance the software, providing alternative or additional means of input and output. In other cases, they will be useful adjuncts to the programs. Speech input and output will make software far more user-friendly. They will remove the artificial constraints imposed by our current necessity for relying on literate rather than oral interaction. They will also eradicate the artificial divisions that computers presently impose between the different language modes. Often in learning activities away from the computer, all the language arts are seen to interrelate. Technical constraints prevent this on a computer. There will also be a number of occasions when speech synthesis and recognition will be integral to the software's aims. Reading programs will become far more valuable if a speech component can be incorporated.

The addition of a speech component to software will dramatically increase the attraction of interaction with a computer. Input and output are likely to be hastened, and exchanges between users and machine will be more dynamic. Care will need to be taken in how this oral interaction is managed. Because of technological constraints, the oral component of this interaction will be one-way at the outset. Only speech synthesis will be implemented on early machines and so problems of user response will be encountered. In speech-accompanied software, the presentation of a number of voiced answers, after each of which users are prompted to indicate on a keyboard whether the answer is correct or not, is a way around one of the problems surrounding spoken interaction at the moment.

Even when speech input becomes a reality, multiple choice answers will still be useful as models for users to emulate in forming their own replies. The multiple choice format works best, however, when the whole menu is presented before any selection is made. Oral multiple choice menus will involve a memory retention factor that is absent from graphic representations of language. Because of the sequential nature of speech, the use of multiple choice techniques demanding memory retention may be no bad thing. They might help to develop the listening habit among hearers. However, there may be times when the interplay of memory skills will obscure or confuse the activity being encouraged. This might be more true of longer spoken units than of small sets of phonemes or words. At times it might be better for an audial presentation to be a single direct question requiring only a straightforward answer to it. More complex forms of audial interaction might be better introduced once users have developed reading skills. Then multiple audial presentations can be accompanied by their written forms to remind users of their choices.

As far as developing higher order oracy skills is concerned, computers can and will have little to offer unless use is made of their interactive facility. Other audio-visual resources are vastly superior in their quality of output. The computer scores only in its ability to manipulate speech in response to user input. This will come into its own when we have achieved greater perfection in speech synthesis. In the meantime, the interfacing of a random access disk player with a computer to control and manipulate the speech it contains can still offer a powerful learning tool. This interfacing can provide structured language learning and practice situations including aural comprehension activities. Even video and sound tape, with their sequential storage and retrieval of information, might have a place. While random access devices allow a computer to be flexible in the way it presents language and to have recourse to reinforcement loops or parallel sound tracks, there is also a place for more sophisticated language learners to be offered only a single exposure to the audio material.

Using some form of speech production, users can be offered narrations of considerable length. These need not be serial, but could develop according to listener dictates or performance on some inbuilt computer task. Comprehension answers can be keyed in with the computer acting upon these in what it retrieves and produces next. Some commercial 'interactive' fiction neatly presents audio stories on cassette to be followed by a range of computer activities using the screen and keyboard to monitor listener comprehension.

The issue of user input as opposed to computer output of speech at this sustained level of verbal utterance is more problematic. We have already noted that computer recognition of speech is still some way behind its ability to produce speech. Unfortunately, too, we cannot turn in the meantime towards other peripheral devices to use instead, as we can with computer synthesis of speech. We can, however, predict some possible future developments from the work already undertaken on speech recognition by computers in restricted domains. The way such systems process language is by a concentration on specific words rather than on the whole utterance. This may have potential in language development if teachers are prepared to accept the restricted domains within which these systems operate. After all, much language – especially that to be found in a classroom – is task oriented. Provided that the concept of restricted domains can be adapted to provide with ease a large number of such domains, or one sufficiently comprehensive one, then it might be possible to see such software running on micro-computers with expanded memory stores.

We can take an example of this software at a fairly restricted level of oral expression. The computer begins by presenting a series of images relating a story. The images could be accompanied by an audial narration consisting of single sentences. Users are expected to repeat these, and the computer monitors their expression. Later, the visual images are repeated, and users are asked to supply their own narration without any audial prompts. This time the computer does not match users' vocal input against its own speech data, since there will be considerable differences of vocabulary, word order, stress and intonation. Instead, the computer would look for key words in the users' narration. Making the software even more interactive, the story might be accompanied by questions in the sound channel. The computer would then look for specific words in the answers before continuing. If it does not find them then it would ask further questions or repeat part of the story. The answers spoken by users could be stored by the computer as the basis of a spoken composition. This could then be replayed or used as the basis upon which further software could be designed to operate. Developments of this software could encourage sustained logical thought and consistency.

In time, computer users might be able to enter into real dialogues with a computer. Imagine a narrative where the computer asks users specific questions about the narrative and then displays (textually or in graphic form) the developing story on screen. When this facility can be linked to an expert system, then users will be able to enter into meaningful dialogues with computers. It is already possible to interrogate a computer through a typewritten question-and-answer routine. When this facility becomes available as an oral exchange, the effects could be profound. Even illiterate users will have access to information and powerful means of processing it. All users might find their perceptions, thought processes and oral skills challenged in ways we do not yet realise when they converse with the inhuman, but fast, logical and immensely knowledgeable memory processes of a computer.

Perhaps one can foresee a time when the visual component of software is replaced entirely by an audial component. Computers would then become very different machines. We already confuse the central microprocessor hidden away inside a computer case with the keyboard and video display unit. These are only two modes of interaction between the central processing unit and its users. They are not part of the computer itself. Imagine a box with just a listening microphone and talking speaker instead. Such devices could present us with a post-literate communications system. They would force us to re-adopt many of the skills rehearsed more adequately in the days before printing developed. Our listening skills would certainly be heightened. Hopefully, though, we would also overcome some of the problems we would encounter through a greater degree of oral and audial interaction with a patient and understanding machine.

Our listening skills may soon be taxed by computers. It is likely that the first widespread use we see of computerised speech will be in synthesised prompt statements for the range of software that already exists. The quality of speech will be poor, but users' persistence in trying to distinguish the sounds emanating from the machines might actually foster listening powers. Much later, software designers will perhaps begin to explore the true potential of oral interaction and to realise its advantageous idiosyncrasies. At that time, teachers of the language arts will really begin to see how oracy can be developed with microcomputers – if only to cope with the demands the machines make.

Such things are largely in the future, however. In order to see how a microcomputer can develop talking and listening skills today, teachers must look further afield.

Computers and oral exchanges

It is rare for students in school to work individually with a micro-computer. This is partly a matter of expediency, given the ratio of pupils to computers in most classes. Partly, though, it might also result from a teacher's belief in the value of group work and a wish to ensure that individual users maintain human contact while interacting with a machine.

Some software is expressly designed for multiple users. It might counter one user against another as competitors in the completion of some task. It might ask users to act in role as part of a simulation exercise or simply to discuss and collaborate in the running of a program. In these situations, a computer can be used to create a language environment around itself, and there can be as much pupil-to-pupil exchange as there is pupil-to-machine; probably more. In some circumstances, the computer might not even remain the focus of the group. It might simply stimulate or structure a group's activity, rather in the way that Douglas Barnes has suggested,[1] if group work conducted for the sake of discussion is to have cohesion, direction and purpose.

To consider a few examples, a computer may be programmed to act as a catalyst stimulating response; it may become consultant to a group acting as 'resident expert' called upon at any time during the discussion; it may act as a confidant, allowing users to explore hypotheses without intimidation; it may act as chairman, focussing discussion, prompting new lines of enquiry, moving the conversation forward; or it may act as critic, monitoring and assessing performance. As the search for new ways of using a limited resource with large numbers of pupils continues, further expansion of the possibilities is likely. The use of a computer for role play is a strong contender since computer simulation is now well established.

There are many programs that might serve as examples. Since microcomputers are so often used by small groups rather than individuals, virtually all software generates some form of speech work. Increasingly, however, there are programs specifically published to aid discussion and decision-making processes. In the language arts, a number of simulations and fantasy games all involve decision-making, many of them complex. Adventure games are probably the best known. The discussion that develops is as much concerned with learning the limited command vocabulary that the machine understands as with pursuing the ultimate quest of the adventure. The fact that the games concern imaginative situations calling for empathy and sensitivity to character and situation heightens the discussion that results. Another advantage of this type of software is that the computer allows users to follow through actions and see the result of their decisions.

All group uses of a microcomputer involve it in discourse to a greater or lesser degree. Many of them, while awarding the computer a powerful role, do not actually involve it in the discourse that develops. In such cases, a computer develops the language environment around itself but it is not an active member of the ensuing exchanges. In terms of quality of utterance and manipulatory power over discourse, a computer may be a significant but not necessarily large user of language itself. This does not alter the fact that the language generated owes its creation and sustenance to the computer's presence. Other media can be used to stimulate discussion but few can also continue to prompt, guide or sustain it once it is in progress. The level and intensity of speech around a computer owe much to the nature of the machine.

Computers and discourse

We have not yet begun to exploit the potential of the computer for oral work in schools. To do so we need to be much clearer about the nature of the discussion that can and does go on around a computer when it is placed in a classroom. In order to understand the type of language contexts in which a microcomputer might now be placed, linguistic models of analysis might be appropriate. This will be taking us away from immediate concerns, but it is important that teachers of the language arts are clear about how computers might be, and already are being, used in classrooms.

The use of linguistic analyses could perform a double function: they ought to clarify the precise nature (and value) of the verbal discourse surrounding group use of a microcomputer; and they might have a far more specific use enabling clarification of the way in which language is here being used for learning. The application of discourse analysis techniques to group situations around a computer is obvious. However, we also have much to learn if we apply the same techniques to the more specific interaction between a computer and its user(s) – even if that exchange is not yet oral.

Computers are not passive. Even as repositories of information they are interactive and require, typically, a form of linguistic input or response via a keyboard. It would be wrong to assume that this typewritten form of interaction always obeys the conventions of written modes. Even though computers and humans do not yet interact orally, a computer display is often more like the transcript of a verbal exchange with its less formalised and syntactically structured characteristics. The speed with which a computer can display written statements in response to a user's stimulus belies the tardiness characteristic of the written medium while user input is often facilitated by the use of keystrokes so that the immediacy of oral exchanges is further approached. Users anthropomorphise computers: students of all ages talk to computers even if the machines cannot yet answer back. There is no true verbal discourse, but the interaction involved between computer and user seems to relate more to verbal exchanges than to written communication; and it can be explored as such to reveal interesting facts about how computers already use oral language strategies.

Verbal interaction inside classrooms tends to differ markedly from desultory conversation in that its main purpose is to question, instruct and inform. The difference is reflected in the nature of the exchange. In normal conversation, topic changes are unpredictable and uncontrollable. Inside a classroom, it is one of the functions of the teacher to choose the topic, decide how it will be subdivided into smaller units and cope with digressions and misunderstandings. Exactly how a teacher does so has received considerable attention over the last 30 years. A program must be highly structured with defined parameters and, in this, much software follows precisely the teaching pattern identified by analysts like Sinclair.[2]

In computer assisted instruction (CAI), a computer guides the user towards some educational objectives by means of a dialogue. The computer prompts an input response from the user and then checks, evaluates and comments upon the response before moving the dialogue forward in a predetermined direction and prompting a new response. The computer, like the teacher in the classroom, is essentially in control of the situation; in order to control the student successfully, it asks questions and provides the student with information depending upon the answers to those questions.

Question/answer exchanges are only one possible form of natural language interaction with a computer, but they are certainly common. This is only to be expected. The software emulates the direct and formal teacher/pupil relationships found in many classrooms. Whether this emulation was intentional (as was possible in Japan and the United States, where designers looked on computers as teacher substitutes), or whether it arose from the very nature of machine interaction with humans and programming techniques, is debatable. Whatever the reasons, CAI discourse is similar to that found in formal classrooms and is thus susceptible to similar forms of descriptive analysis.

Sinclair's model of analysis was devised for, and applied to, a particular formalised mode of discourse between pupil and teacher, one which centres on alternating teacher stimulus and pupil response. It shows how, through language, various learning possibilities can be opened and closed to pupils. Many teachers today would start from the proposition that language is a means of learning, and so it is only through active participation using language themselves that pupils can really learn. Douglas Barnes has explored general issues in the relationship between language and learning. He has formulated a model of analysis that in application shows that many teachers' linguistic strategies consist of a narrow range of choices taken with almost monotonous regularity from a much broader spectrum of possible language uses. For example, Barnes distinguishes between closed questions having only one acceptable answer and open questions where the parameters are less well defined and where a number of different answers are acceptable. In some circumstances even factual questions may be open to a variety of responses. Reasoning questions, too, may be open or closed: reasoning questions may consist of recall of required knowledge from memory; open reasoning accepts a variety of possible responses. Closed questions are far easier to program and yet linguists ponder the effect on discourse when questions are asked without a genuine desire for information. This must have significance for computer interaction with a learner.

Barnes also identifies social utterances, which typically consist of control questions imposing a speaker's wish upon his or her receiver, and appeal questions, which seek a recipient's agreement and collaboration in the sharing of an experience. These matters are important in the structuring and manipulation of a computer program to interact with pupils. So too is Barnes's concern with the way a teacher deals with inappropriate input to lessons. This includes whether pupils are required to express personal responses of perception, feeling and attitude or not; how large a part they take in a lesson; how pupils' input shows their success in following a lesson and so forth.

Implicit in much of this is the fact that language is used for the maintenance of social relationships. Barnes asks how the relationship between teacher and pupil is manifested in language. He asks if there is any observable distinction between the language of instruction and the language of relationships. Is the language of relationships intimate or formal? Does it vary during the discourse?

Barnes's work provides a descriptive model for a precise analysis of language interaction with a microcomputer. In addition, it raises some interesting strategies for future programmers to consider, and its application will become even more relevant when computers and users communicate orally. Some of the language techniques discussed would be difficult to incorporate into software. If, however, they are worthwhile, their exclusion might help teachers realise the limitations of computers or of specific programs in certain learning processes. It might be that those same strategies could still find a place if software is not seen separated from its classroom context. Rather it should be viewed as part of a broader educational programme in which software is only one element; a programme in which there will be other resources and teacher/pupil, pupil/pupil language contexts.

We are now moving away from the specific oracy skills that teachers of the language arts will wish to teach in their classrooms. But we have not moved away from their immediate interests and responsibilities as far as language is concerned. Teachers of the language arts need to be aware of the ways microcomputers can be programmed to use language and of the demands that this use might make upon students. The work of researchers like Sinclair and Barnes might help them meet this need.

Computers as language users across the curriculum: a postscript

Computers can be programmed to appear complex language users. They can be commanded to utilise written language in a highly literate way; they can be commanded to participate (though not yet orally) in spoken discourse that they have stimulated among their users. They may also act as hybrid systems, capable of utilising a variety of media for communication, of initiating a diversity of communication processes and of performing various roles in communication acts. They demand attention whether or not language arts teachers think they can help them in their teaching. It has been a recurring argument of this book that language teachers have a duty to equip their students with the necessary skills they will need in an electronic society. Even today, students will already need the skills to cope with computer encounters elsewhere in the curriculum.

It is now widely accepted that the role of language is of crucial importance to the learning process as a means of communicating ideas and of internalising and organising experiences. Since microcomputers can be employed as a linguistic medium of communication right across the curriculum, they raise further questions concerning the nature and relationship of language and learning. Text on a visual display screen prompts questions on the perception of written symbols. Verbal input requires precise spelling rules (often demanded at a very early age) and keyboard accuracy. The use of a computer as an information retrieval system provokes discussion of the study and research skills necessary for handling written source materials. The strategies of interaction summon thoughts on the language strategies to be employed in learning processes. There may even be new, and as yet unrealised, linguistic issues given the singularity and originality of the medium.

In language and learning research, the nature of the subject – the mode of communication or medium to be explored – is relatively easy to identify and isolate. It then becomes susceptible to specific forms of analysis: readability studies of the written word or discourse analysis of verbal transactions, for example. Microcomputers can appear complex multiple users of language, often creating around themselves a plethora of language environments. The machines become amenable to many different forms of language analysis, often at the same time. At other times, a computer's language demands may be susceptible to none we have yet devised.

Teachers of the language arts have an important role to play. They should bring their knowledge of the subject to bear on the way computers are used linguistically. This should be of interest to their teaching colleagues using computers across the curriculum, to programmers and to hardware designers. But also, in their own classrooms, language teachers should be helping their pupils acquire the skills they need. This will involve awareness of microcomputers today across the curriculum, and tomorrow in the society that these students will enter. Some of the language skills required will demand the introduction of a microcomputer or other electronic device into language arts classes. Once introduced however, teachers are likely to find that even the present language arts curriculum can benefit from the presence of a microcomputer. Hopefully, the foregoing pages have given some indication how.

References

Introduction

1. Chomsky, N., review of Skinner's *Verbal Behaviour* in *Language 35*, No. 1, 1959.

2. Computers and reading

1. Gattegno, C., *Towards a Visual Culture*, Outerbridge & Dienstfrey, New York, 1969, pp. 71–2.
2. Ibid., pp. 70–1.
3. Baker, K., quoted by O'Grady, C., in 'Untried computers for the very young' *The Times Educational Supplement*, 23 July 1982, p. 8.
4. Gattegno, C., op. cit., p. 73.
5. Sherrington, R., *Television and Language Skills*, Oxford University Press, 1973.
6. Moore, O. K., 'About talking typewriters, folk models and discontinuties: a progress report on twenty years of research, development and application in *Educational Technology*, Vol. 20, No. 2, 1980, p. 27.
7. Millerson, G., *The Techniques of Television Production*, Chaucer Press, 1972, p. 354.
8. Tinker, M. A. and Patterson, D. G., 'Influence of type form on speed of reading' in *Journal of Applied Psychology*, Vol. 12, August 1928, p. 359.
9. Harrison, M. F. and Braverman, B. B., 'Legibility factors related to the captioning of video displays', unpublished.
10. Jones, D. F., 'Teletext in the primary school' in *Visual Education*, August/September 1979, p. 35.
11. Fedida, S. and Malik, R., *The Viewdata Revolution*, Associated Business Press, 1979, p. 15.
12. Whitehead, F. *et al.*, *Children's Reading Interests*, Evans/Methuen, 1975, p. 40.
13. McLuhan, M., *Understanding Media*, Routledge & Kegan Paul, 1964, p. 82.

3.   Computers and writing

1. Baecker, R. M., 'Human computer systems: a state-of-the-art review' in Koles, P. A., Wrolstad, M. E. and Bouma, M., eds, *The Processing of Visible Language*, Vol. 2, Plenum Press, New York, 1980, p. 430.
2. Geoffrion, L. and Bergerson, D., *Caris*, University of New Hampshire, 1976.
3. Papert, S., *Mindstorms: Children, Computers and Powerful Ideas*, Harvester Press, 1980, p. 49.
4. Chomsky, N., *Syntactic Structures*, Mouton, The Hague, 1957.
5. Raphael, B., *The Thinking Computer*, W. H. Freeman, San Francisco, 1976, pp. 189ff.
6. Johns, T. F., 'The use of an analytic generator' in *The ESP Teacher* (EFL Documents), British Council, 1982, p. 7.
7. Kowalski, R., *LOGIC as a Computer Language for Children*, Imperial College, London, 1982, p. 1.
8. De Bono, E., quoted in the *Sunday Times*, 20 March 1983.
9. Winchester, S., 'At the outset was the word' in the *Sunday Times*, 28 November 1982.
10. Papert, S., op. cit., p. 30.
11. Wallace, I., *The Writing of One Novel*, Simon & Schuster, New York, 1968, p. 21.
12. Garner, A., 'A bit more practice' in Meek, M., *et al.*, eds., *The Cool Web*, Bodley Head, 1977, p. 198.
13. Wallace, I., op. cit., p. 21.
14. Fowles, J., 'Notes on an unfinished novel' in Bradbury, M., *The Novel Today*, Fontana 1977, pp. 126–8.
15. Pearce, P., 'Writing a book: *A Dog So Small*' in Blishen, E., ed., *The Thorny Paradise*, Kestrel, 1975, pp. 140–1.
16. Pearce, P., op. cit., pp. 136–8.
17. Kermode, F., *How We Read Novels*, University of Southampton, 1975, p. 15.
18. Eco, U., quoted in Kermode, F., op. cit. p. 17.

4.   Computers and oracy

1. Barnes, D. and Todd, F., *Communation and Learning in Small Groups*, Routledge & Kegan Paul, 1977.
2. Sinclair, J., *et al.*, *The English Used by Teachers and Pupils*, University Birmingham, 1972.

Glossary

allophone the speech sub-components combined to produce spoken words.

analog(ue) data represented by a continuously variable physical quality such as voltage or angular position.

cathode ray tube (CRT) see **visual display unit**.

CAL computer assisted learning.

central processing unit (CPU) main constituent of a computer, consisting of an immediate access store, arithmetic unit and control unit.

column the number of columns or character spaces per line of a visual display units; usually 20, 40, or 80.

compact audio disk flat, circular storage device for sound from which data is read at random by a laser beam tracking across the surface.

computer a machine that, under the control of a stored program, automatically accepts, stores and manipulates data.

cursor a character (usually flashing) that indicates the current display position on a visual display unit.

data bank collection of databases or large files of data.

database collection of structured data.

data file organised collection of related records normally stored on disk or tape in a form acceptable for input to a computer system for processing.

data processing operation of collecting information, processing it and presenting results.

dedicated system a computer system used for a single application.

dialect a version of a programming language specific to one particular computer range or model.

dictionary chip a **ROM** containing information for computer generation of specific spoken words.

disk see **floppy**, **compact** or **video**.

disk drive hardware device for retrieving information from a random access floppy disk.

EPROM see **ROM**.

external memory store memory unit that might be attached to a computer and can be referred to for instructions or for data such as text.

floppy disk storage device consisting of a flat, circular plate coated with magnetic material. Data is written to and read from a set of concentric tracks in random fashion.

graph plotter output device that draws lines on paper.

graphics the representation of information by computer on a visual display unit in graphical form. Here it also refers to animated sequences and to the display of shapes specifically defined by software and not part of the machine's character set.

graphics tablet input device where the movement of a pen over a sensitive pad is translated into digital signals giving the pen's position.

hard copy computer output printed on paper instead of on screen.

hardware the various electronic items of equipment that make up a computer system.

high level programming language a problem-oriented language, approximating ordinary English syntax, in which instructions to a computer may be equivalent to several machine code commands.

high resolution graphics graphical display units capable of fine definition by plotting in excess of 250 distinct pixel points in the width of the screen; also the graphics thus produced.

input device peripheral unit that can accept data, presented in an appropriate machine-readable form, decode it and transmit it as electrical pulses to a central processing unit.

interface hardware and software required between a central processing unit and peripheral device to compensate for the differences in their operating characteristics.

internal memory store part of a computer where data and program instructions are held or stored.

joystick convenient form of analogue-to-digital converter where input is the movement of a control lever in two dimensions.

key word a single term in a programming language dialect signalling a particular command to a computer.

keystroke command or other input to a computer signalled by the depression of a single key.

light-pen input device used in conjunction with a visual display unit. The hardware senses the position of the pen and relays this information to the central processor.

list linearly ordered data structure.

listing display on screen or as hard copy of program statements or data in sequence.

loading the transfer of instructions and data to computer memory from an external source.

low resolution graphics graphical display of limited definition (80 horizontal picture points or fewer) and where simple pictures are often built up by plotting relatively large blocks or by using special graphics characters.

machine code a code that represents the basic instructions a computer can recognise and execute without any intermediate translation.

memory that part of a computer where data and instructions are held.

microcomputer in essence a microprocessor that, under control of a stored program, automatically accepts and processes data and supplies results of that processing (see also **computer**).

microprocessor a single silicon chip that performs the functions of a central processing unit.

mouse a tracking device for moving the cursor on screen by running the device over a desk-top surface.

output device a peripheral unit that translates pulses from a computer into a human readable form or into a form for reprocessing by a computer at a later stage.

paddle hand-held control device often used in computer games.

peripheral device any input, output or back-up storage device that can be connected to a central processor.

program a complete set of commands structured so as to specify an algorithm that a computer can accept and execute.

program statement usually a source language instruction that generates several machine code instructions.

programming language an artificial language constructed so that humans and programmable machines can communicate with each other in a precise and intelligible way.

radio frequency (RF) the typical wave signal by which broadcast television is transmitted. The signal is not as clear or faithful as a video signal.

random access a system of gaining access to information whereby any record of information can be found with equal efficiency and ease.

restricted domain a specified field of knowledge or limited situation in which a computer under program control is defined to work.

ROM (Read Only Memory) memory that may not be written to by a programmer. The software in the ROM is fixed during manufacture. PROM (Programmable ROM) is a type of ROM where the program may be written after manufacture but is then fixed. EPROM (Erasable PROM) is a type of PROM memory that can be erased by a special process and written as for a new PROM.

speech recognition the process of analysing a spoken utterance and comparing it with those known to a computer system.

speech synthesis an output device that generates sound similar to human speech on receipt of digital signals.

string lexical data in the form of a list of characters.

teletex generic name for technique of transmitting textual data between computer terminals.

teletext computer-based information retrieval system using screen messages broadcast by television.

touch screen a screen with sensors around the perimeter to identify and locate the position of a finger or pointer touching the screen.

touchpad a pressure-sensitive peripheral input device.

video disk storage device consisting of a flat, circular plate coated with magnetic material. Data is written to and read from a set of concentric tracks in random fashion.

video monitor a device for the presentation of computer output in the form of text or graphics. Similar to a television screen but normally accepts a video signal rather than radio frequency, and thus capable of better picture definition and screen legibility.

video player a device for the random access playback of sound and pictures stored on video disk.

viewdata information retrieval system using conventional telephone network to gain on-line access to range of national and international host computers.

viewtex see **teletex**.

visual display unit (VDU) terminal device incorporating a cathode ray tube on which text and graphics can be displayed.

Select bibliography

Adams, A. and Jones, E., *Teaching Humanities in the Microelectronics Age*, Open University Press, 1983.

Ahl, D., 'Computers in language arts' in Lecarme, O. and Lewis, R., *Computers and Education*, North Holland Publishing Co., 1975.

Appleby, B., 'Computers and composition: an overview' in *Focus*, Vol. 9, No. 3, Spring 1983.

Barron, I. and Curnow, R., *The Future with Microelectronics*, Open University Press, 1979.

Botha, J. J., 'Computer-based education and the teaching of English for specific purposes: report on a project in progress' in *System*, Vol. 10(3), 1982.

Boyd, G., Keler, A. and Kemner, R., 'Remedial and second language teaching using CAL' in Smith, P., ed., *Proceedings of the CAL '81 Symposium*, Pergamon Press, 1982.

Bradley, V., 'Improving students' writing with microcomputers' in *Language Arts*, Vol. 59, No. 7, October 1982.

Briggs, B. and Meredith, M., *Electronic Learning Aids: Enquiry Two*, Council for Educational Technology, 1983.

Centre of Information on Language Teaching and Research (CILT), *Computers, Language and Language Learning*, Information Guide 22, 1982.

CILT/Council for Educational Technology, *New Technological Developments for Language Teaching and Learning* (composite report), CILT, 1982.

Chandler, D., *Exploring English with Microcomputers*, Council for Educational Technology, 1983.

'I don't know what to write' in *Educational Computing*, November 1982, p. 24.

'Microcomputers and the English teacher' in Terry, C., ed., *Using Microcomputers in Schools*, Croom Helm, 1984.

'The games some pupils play' in *Educational Computing*, Vol. 12(10), November 1981.

'The potential of the microcomputer in the English classroom' in Adams, A., ed., *New Directions in English Teaching*, Falmer Press, 1982.

Using Computers in English: A Practical Guide, Methuen, 1984.

Young Learners and the Microcomputer, Oxford University Press, 1984.

Chandler, D. and Marcus, S., eds., *Computers and Literacy*, Open University Press, 1985.

Chapman, B. L. and Wilby, J. F., 'Language and silence (deaf children)' in *Computers in Schools*, Vol. 4(93), March 1982.

Collins, A., *Teaching Reading and Writing with Personal Computers*, Bolt, Beranek & Newman, Cambridge, Massachusetts, 1983.

Collins, A., Bruce, B. and Rubin, A., 'Microcomputer-based writing activities for the upper elementary grades' in *Proceedings of the Fourth International Learning Technology Congress and Exposition*, Society for Applied Learning Technology, Orlando, Florida, 1982.

Daiute, C., *Computers and Writing*, Addison Wesley, 1982.

'Writing, creativity and change' in *Childhood Education*, March/April 1983.

Davies, G. and Higgins, J., *Computers, Language and Language Learning*, CILT/Baker Book Services, 1982.

Demaizière, F., 'Experiments in CAL of English grammar at University of Paris' in *Proceedings of the CAL '81 Symposium*, Pergamon Press, 1982.

Edwards, D. B., 'The use of natural language computers in the teaching of English on the secondary level', MSc. thesis, Southern Connecticut State College, 1973.

Evans, C., *The Mighty Micro*, Gollancz, 1979.

Fedida, S. and Malik, R., *The Viewdata Revolution*, Associated Business Press, 1979.

Frase, L. T., *Computer Aids for Text Editing and Design* (papers presented at annual meeting of American Educational Research Association, Boston, April 1980), Bell Laboratories, Piscataway, NJ, 1980.

Futcher, D., 'US package scores points – review of American package "Wordwatch"' in *Educational Computing*, January 1982.

Garland, R., ed., *Microcomputers and Children in the Primary School*, Falmer Press, 1982.

Geoffrion, L. D. and Olga P., *Computers and Reading Instruction*, Addison Wesley, 1983.

Godfrey, W., 'Score: successes 1; disasters 1 – CAL and the teaching of English fundamentals to university level students' in *Proceedings of the Third Canadian Symposium on Instrumental Technology*, February 1980.

Gray, T. and Blease, D., 'Creator of contents for language work' in *Educational Computing*, December 1981.

Greenfield, P. M., *Mind and Media: The Effects of Television, Computers and Video Games*, Fontana, 1984.

Hammond, R., *The Writer and the Word Processor*, Coronet, 1984.

Hawkins, J., Sheingold, K., Gearhart, M. and Berger, C., *Microcomputers in Schools: Impact on the Social Life of Elementary Classrooms*, Center for Children and Technology, Bank Street College of Education, New York, 1982.

Hawthorne, D., 'Microcomputers in English teaching' in *Computer Age*, August 1980, pp. 28–30.

Higgins, J., *Computers and English Language Teaching: British Council Inputs*, British Council, 1982.

'Computers and the teaching of English as a second language' in *Proceedings of the Education Computing Conference*, North London Polytechnic, April 1982.

'Computers in language training' in *Language Training 1982 in Computers and ELT*, British Council, 1982.

'How real is a computer simulation?' in *ELT Documents: 113 Humanistic Approaches in Language Teaching*, British Council, December 1981.

'The intelligent blackboard' in *Media Education Development*, Vol. 15(3), September 1982.

Higgins, J. and Johns, T., *Computers in Language Learning*, Collins ELT, 1984.

Hills, P., *The Future of the Printed Word*, Open university Press, 1980.

Irving, A., *Infostorms*, Council for Educational Technology, 1984.

Jones, T., *Microelectronics and Society*, Open University Press, 1980.

Kidd, M. and Holmes, G., 'The computer and language remediation' in *PLET*, August 1982.

Knott, R., *The English Department in a Changing World*, Open University Press, 1985.

Last, R. and King, P., 'The design and implementation of a computer assisted learning package for modern language teaching: a research progress report' in *British Journal of Educational Technology*, Vol. 10(3), October 1979.

Lawler, R., *One Child's Learning: Introducing Writing with a Computer*, AI Memo No. 575, Logo Memo No. 56, Artificial Intelligence Laboratory, Massachusetts Institute of Technology, March 1980.

Lawlor, J., ed., *Computers in Composition Instruction*, Educational Research and Development, Los Alamos, California, 1982.

Longworth, N., 'We're moving into the information society. What shall we teach the children?' in *Computer Education*, June 1981.

Marcus, S., 'Compupoem: a computer assisted writing activity' in *English Journal*, February 1982.

'Compupoem: CAI for writing and studying poetry' in *The Computing Teacher*, March 1982.

'The muse and the machine: a computers and poetry project' in *Classroom Computer News*, Vol. 3, No. 2, November/December 1982.

Marcus, S. and Blau, S., 'Not seeing is relieving: invisible writing with computers' in *Educational Technology*, April 1983.

Mason, G., Blanchard, J. S. and Daniel, B. *Computer Applications in Reading*, International Reading Association, Newark, Delaware, 1983.

Moore, P., *Computers in English*, forthcoming (Methuen, 1986).

Northeast Regional Exchange, *Teaching Writing through Technology – a Resource Guide*, Northeast Regional Exchange, Chelmsford, Massachusetts, 1983.

Papert, S., *Mindstorms: Children, Computers and Powerful Ideas*, Harvester Press, 1980.

Robinson, B., 'Reading and the video screen' in *Media in Education Research*, Working Paper 2, University of Southampton, 1983; reprinted in *British Journal of Educational Technology*, Vol. 16, No. 1, January 1985.

Rubin, A., 'The computer confronts language arts' in Wilkinson, A., ed., *Classroom Computers and Cognitive Science*, Academic Press, New York, 1982.

Scratcherd, T., Smith, I. and Langham, R., 'Clarity is all for school computing (remedial English and typing)' in *Practical Computing*, Vol. 5, Issue 2, February 1982.

Sharples, M., 'A computer-based writing scheme for creative writing' in Lewis, R. and Tagg, D., eds., *Computers and Education*, North Holland Publishing Co., 1981.

'Microcomputers and creative writing' in Howe, J. and Ross, P., eds., *Microcomputers in Secondary Education*, Routledge & Kegan Paul, 1981.

Poetry from LOGO, Working Paper No. 30, Department of Artificial Intelligence, University of Edinburgh, June 1978.

Using a Computer to Develop Written Style, Working Paper No. 54, Department of Artificial Intelligence, University of Edinburgh, June 1979.

Short, J. and Brown, R., 'The applications of microcomputers to English essay writing' in proceedings of Conference *Involving Micros in Education*, Lancaster University, March 1982.

Smith, F., 'Demonstrations, engagements and sensitivity: the choice between people and programs' in *Language Arts*, Vol. 58, No. 6, September 1981.

The Promise and Threat of Microcomputers in Language Education, Centre for the Teaching of Reading, Reading University, in conjunction with Abel Press, Victoria, BC, 1985.

Terrell, C. D. and Linyard, O., 'Evaluation of electronic learning aids: Texas Instruments' speak and spell' in *International Journal of Man–Machine Studies*, 17, 1982.

Thompson, V., 'Videotex in education' in *Media Education Development*, Vol. 15(3), September 1982.

Ward, R., 'Computer assisted learning and deaf children's language' in *Teaching Deaf*, Vol. 6(6), November 1982.

Watson, D., 'Computer assisted learning in the humanities', Proceedings of IFIP World Conference, Lausanne, 1981, in Lewis, R. and Tagg, D., eds., *Computers in Education*, North Holland Publishing Co., 1981.

Windeatt, S. A., 'A project in self-access learning for English language and study skills (CML)' in *Practical Papers in English Language Education*, Vol. 3, 1980.

Wresch, W., ed., *The Computer in Composition Instruction*, National Council for Teachers of English (NCTE), 1984.

Zacchei, D., 'The adventures and exploits of the dynamic storymaker and textman' in *Classroom Computer News*, May/June 1982.

Index